Praise for

Out of Darkness and Into the Light

Denise Shick does not shy away from addressing the confusion surrounding gender identity while remaining deeply rooted in Scripture. Her book challenges readers to confront societal narratives with the truth of God's Word, urging a return to honoring Christ as Creator. *Out of Darkness into the Light* is a must-read for anyone seeking to understand gender identity from a biblical perspective and to rediscover the joy of living in alignment with God's purpose.

She eloquently sheds light on gender identity confusion and provides a nuanced understanding of the misguided paths that people have taken. Through her insightful exploration, she reveals how God cannot only restore and transform fractured identities but also heal past wounds. With His grace, she encourages a future filled with hope and possibility.

In a world of uncertainty, this book stands as a beacon of truth, beckoning the reader to recognize and embrace the masterpiece of God's Divine Creation. This book is highly recommended for those ultimately eager to deepen their understanding of God's design for humanity.

—JAMES E. PHELAN, LCSW, BCD, MBA, PsyD
Secretary, *Association of Christians in Health & Human Services* (ACHHS)
Author and Adjunct Professor

Out of the Darkness into the Light is an excellent resource for those struggling to understand transgenderism from a biblical perspective. Denise does a superb job of equipping the believer to speak more intelligently about this issue.

—MARC S. DILLWORTH, PhD
Licensed Psychotherapist, specializing in gender identity issues

In this rare, insightful book, Denise Shick exposes the insidious lies causing *gender confusion* in our culture. Parents, grandparents, and those seeking truth about the transgender world will gain a firm grasp on God's "divine design" for the only two sexes He created—male and female. Moreso, you will learn how to refute misconceptions with both scientific and biblical truth, while others will be personally empowered to turn away from their own gender confusion.

Because Denise grew up with a troubled transgender father, she knows firsthand the devastating consequences of acting on the false beliefs permeating our society. Thank you, Denise, your book is nothing short of heroic.

—June Hunt
Founder & CSO (Chief Servant Officer)
Hope for the Heart & The Hope Center
Author of *Homosexuality & SSA: The Struggle with Same Sex Attraction, How to Forgive When You Don't Feel Like It, Counseling Through Your Bible Handbook*

OUT OF DARKNESS AND INTO THE LIGHT

Winning the Battle of Gender Identity

DENISE SHICK

Out of Darkness and into the Light by Denise Shick © 2024

All Scripture quotations, unless otherwise indicated, are taken from the Holy Bible, New International Version®, NIV®. Copyright© 1973, 1978, 1984, 2011 by Biblica, Inc.™ Used by permission of Zondervan. All rights reserved worldwide. www.zondervan.com. "NIV" and "New International Version" are trademarks registered in the United States Patent and Trademark Office by Biblica, Inc.™

Scripture quotations marked AMP are taken from The Amplified® Bible, Copyright© 2015 by The Lockman Foundation. Used by permission. (www.Lockman.org.) All rights reserved.

Scripture quotations marked ESV are taken from The Holy Bible, English Standard Version® (ESV®), Copyright© 2001 by Crossway, a publishing ministry of Good News Publishers. Used by permission. All rights reserved.

Scripture quotations marked MSG are taken from *The Message*. Copyright© by Eugene H. Peterson 1993, 1994, 1995, 1996, 2000, 2001, 2002. Used by permission of Tyndale House Publishers, Inc.

Scripture quotations marked NKJV are taken from the New King James Version. Copyright© 1982 by Thomas Nelson, Inc. Used by permission. All rights reserved.

Scripture quotations marked NLT are taken from the Holy Bible, New Living Translation, copyright©1996, 2004, 2015 by Tyndale House Foundation. Used by permission of Tyndale House Publishers, Inc., Carol Stream, Illinois 60188. All rights reserved.

Scripture quotations marked TLB are taken from The Living Bible, copyright© 1971. Used by permission of Tyndale House Publishers, Inc., Carol Stream, Illinois 60188. All rights reserved.

ISBN: 979-8-9915106-0-8

This book is dedicated to Michael Martinez.

Countless people were blessed by his testimony
of God's great love that changed his life.
Michael was determined to share the gospel
with as many LGTBQ folks as he possibly could.

He was determined for others to hear
what God had done for him by freeing him from
his addiction to alcohol and living a gay life
so they too may have healing.
Michael's passion for others to know that God
has food for their hungry souls will always be
a reminder that faith in God is the answer
to whatever we struggle with.

Michael's favorite verse:

"Seek first his kingdom and his righteousness,
and all these things will be given to you as well."
—Matthew 6:33

CONTENTS

CHAPTER ONE	DIVINE DESIGN	1
CHAPTER TWO	REBELLION	11
CHAPTER THREE	ENVY	19
CHAPTER FOUR	MANIPULATION	27
CHAPTER FIVE	MINIMIZING SIN	41
CHAPTER SIX	GOOD AND EVIL	51
CHAPTER SEVEN	A CRITICAL SPIRIT	61
CHAPTER EIGHT	LIFE OUT OF TRAUMA	71
CHAPTER NINE	EXPOSING THE DARKNESS	83
CHAPTER TEN	LIVING IN THE LIGHT	93

CHAPTER ONE

DIVINE DESIGN

"In the beginning, God created the heavens and the earth."
—Genesis 1:1 ESV

The word *beginning* can be defined as "the act or process of bringing or being brought into being; a start," for example, the beginning of the universe.[1] When God created man and woman at the beginning of creation, He had a plan. He did not make any errors in His creation—including man and woman.

But when humans begin to question God's design, when we allow doubt about His intentions and purposes, we give Satan the opportunity to sweep the foundation, the beginning of all things, from under us.

When people deny biological uniqueness, they strip God of His rights as Creator. The differences in the male and female body are part of His design: "Then the LORD God formed a man from the dust of the ground and breathed into his nostrils the breath of life, and the man became a living being" (Genesis 2:7). God understood Adam needed a helpmate, and Eve was made "fit" for him (Genesis 2:18 ESV). God created Eve as Adam's helper in serving the Triune God and in establishing a family. One person cannot procreate, but together the male and the

---

[1] "Beginning," The Free Dictionary, accessed June 29, 2023, https://www.thefreedictionary.com/beginning.

female can create a family. This is biological fact. Even if a man or woman decides to willingly be sterilized or to have healthy body parts removed to pursue a sinful lifestyle—outside of God's design—both sexes are still needed to procreate. For this reason, there will always be two sexes.

Adam and Eve were free to enjoy life as God's first family unit as long as they respected the Creator's standards of good and evil. God was clear about the consequences of disobedience. Likewise, Adam and Eve were well aware of what would happen if they crossed the line, or better put, ate the forbidden fruit of the Tree of the Knowledge of Good and Evil: "And the LORD God commanded the man, 'You are free to eat from any tree in the garden; but you must not eat from the tree of the knowledge of good and evil, for when you eat from it you will certainly die'" (Genesis 2:16–17).

Like Adam and Eve, each of us is accountable for our decisions and actions. If we accept a lie and live according to it, we will suffer the consequences. Speaking through the serpent, Satan appealed to Adam and Eve with cunning deception: "You will not certainly die. . . . For God knows that when you eat from it [the tree] your eyes will be opened and you will be like God, knowing good and evil" (Genesis 3:4–5). Believing a lie created havoc in Adam and Eve's lives. We will suffer similar consequences if we believe a lie. The serpent went straight to the desires of the flesh with his lie—a lie that still affects us today.

DEFINING TERMS

For the sake of clarity, my use of the word *sex* in this book refers to the biological gender of a male or female. These designations are typically based on four facts:

- Each male and each female possess two sets of chromosomes. The male has what is known as XY chromosomes and the female what is known as XX chromosomes.
- A person's external sexual anatomy
- A person's internal reproductive organs
- The endocrine systems that produce secondary sex characteristics

These facts line up with God's Word—he created male and female—and they match up with human biological science. Any ideologies not based on these facts are falsehoods and deceptions created by humans in an attempt to deny truth. As is the case with all false teaching, these ideologies are rebellion against the Creator.

In our culture, the word *gender* is now used as a social construct, that is "an idea that has been created and accepted by the people in a society."[2] In this sense, gender refers to the psychology, social, and cultural aspects of being male and female. For example, *Merriam-Webster* now lists "having a gender identity that is the opposite of female" as a definition of *male*.[3] A similar definition is listed for *female*. The term *gender identity* describes the psychological aspects associated with being male, female, or neither. *Gender role* describes how males and females are expected to act. But in a world of mass confusion over what is male and female, the model of a gender role is changing.

---

[2] "Social construct," Merriam-Webster Unabridged Dictionary, Online Version, accessed August 7, 2023, https://unabridged.merriam-webster.com/collegiate/social%20construct.

[3] "Male," Merriam-Webster Unabridged Dictionary, Online Version, accessed August 7, 2023, https://unabridged.merriam-webster.com/ collegiate/male.

Transgender men say that a man can become pregnant because these female-to-male transgenders still have female reproductive organs. They can also still menstruate.

GENDER WOVEN INTO OUR DNA

God displayed His magnificent wisdom when He created male and female bodies. Some argue against the biological designations of male and female given above. They seem to believe that if a man takes estrogen and alters his external sexual anatomy, then he will become a woman. Similarly, if a woman takes testosterone and has a double mastectomy, she has become male. But their DNA cannot be changed, so biologically the man is still male and the woman, female.

Our DNA also indicates sex beyond outward appearance and the absence or presence of a Y chromosome. In a study recently conducted by the Weizmann Institute of Science, researchers uncovered thousands of human genes that are expressed—copied out to make proteins—differently in the two sexes.

Pietrokovski and Gershoni investigated further and found there were around 20,000 protein-coding genes. They sorted them by sex, searching for difference in expression in each tissue. The genes with activity biased toward one sex or the other indicated that biological sex also plays a role in preventing specific illness:

1. Some genes expressed only in the left ventricle of the heart of women work to protect their hearts from disease until the women reach menopause.
2. In the liver, another gene processes drugs differently, according to sex.

3. Some genes "highly expressed in the skin of men relative to that in women's skin, and they realized these were related to other growth of body hair."
4. Gene expression for muscle building was higher in men; that for fat storage was higher in women.
5. Another gene was mainly expressed in women and active in the brain. Although its exact function is unknown, the researchers think it may protect the neurons that form Parkinson's—a disease that has a higher prevalence and earlier onset in men.
6. Researchers also "identified gene expression in the liver in women that regulates drug metabolism, providing molecular evidence for the known difference in drug processing between men and women."[4]

All this to say, God really did do what the Word of God says. He created male and female. They are different—uniquely designed to be different by the hand of God.

WHAT ABOUT HERMAPHRODITES?

Without any medical history or proof, some who identify as transgender have suggested they are hermaphrodites—having both male and female characteristics and especially elements of both male and female reproductive organs. Another term for hermaphroditism is intersexuality.

---

[4] "Researchers Identify 6,500 Genes That Are Expressed Differently in Men and Women," American Committee for the Weizmann Institute of Science, May 3, 2017, https://www.weizmann-usa.org/news-media/news-releases/researchers-identify-6-500-genes-that-are-expressed-differently-in-men-and-women.

For example, I testified for six years against proposed bathroom bills before the State of Maryland's House and Senate members in Annapolis. In those hearings, some men suggested they were intersex, but if a House or Senate member asked for a definition of intersex, the men did not say it was a physical condition. They acted as if it was tied to their gender preference and emotional well-being.

Yes, some people are born with male and female genitalia, but this is a rare medical condition. Why does God allow this to happen? We may as well ask why some are born blind or deaf or with severe physical deformities. Matt Slick provides this perspective:

> God's intention of the [sexes] is that those born males act like males and those born females act like females. But, in rare instances, there are babies born with the sexual organs of both sexes. Why is this? First of all, sin is in the world, and it sometimes takes its toll on our bodies, resulting in various deformities. Nevertheless, in the case of hermaphroditism, the identity of the individual is still intended to be one or the other. After all, God would not make someone in contradiction to His created order and purpose. This means the hermaphrodite, thought physically ambiguous, does possess an identity of one or the other. . . . It would seem best left up to knowledgeable and experienced medical staff and parents.[5]

---

[5] Matt Slick, "What about Hermaphrodites?" Christian Apologetics and Research Ministry, Carm.org, December 11, 2008, https://carm.org/about-sexuality/what-about-hermaphrodites/.

In the case of hermaphroditism, God still intends the individual to be either male or female. Many who claim to be hermaphrodites are suffering from gender dysphoria—that is, they are emotionally and mentally distressed about their biological body. Some who identify as transgender are suffering from a spiritual condition rather than a physical one.

WORSHIP: THE DUTY OF ALL HUMANS

The wondrous work of God's hands in creation is beyond what we could imagine. In Psalm 8, David tried to capture his wonder with these words: "When I consider your heavens, the work of your fingers, the moon and the stars, which you have set in place, what is mankind that you are mindful of them, human beings that you care for them?" (vv. 3–4). Like David, we should conclude, "Lord, our Lord, how majestic is your name in all the earth!" (v. 9). We should bow before our majestic God and say, "You are my God!"

We see the perfection of His creation, not with our eyes or mind but with our heart. Our heart alone can discern how absolutely wonderful God's plan for mankind is. Our heart can detect and be grateful for the many blessings He showers on us. Our heart can accept Him as our God.

On the other hand, we can choose the dark lie of the devil that we can be our own god. We can shake our fist at God and say, "I am not a male. I will tell you who I will be." Like the devil, we can choose to rebel against our Creator, or we can choose to worship Him. There are no other choices.

GotQuestions.org provides this insight on worship:

> The Hebrew word translated "worship" literally means "to bow down." In Psalm 5:6, the psalmist uses three different terms to describe bowing down, which is the foundational posture of worship in the Old Testament: "Come, let us *worship* and *bow down*. Let us *kneel* before the Lord our maker" (NLT, emphasis added). Each of the italicized words conveys the image of bowing low, bending the knee, and kneeling. They are meant to inspire the worshiper to bring himself low before God, but physically bowing down is not the true essence of humbling oneself in worship.[6]

The act of bowing down before God is an act of humility, demonstrating our respect for Him as an immeasurably superior being. God made this distinction clear in Exodus 20:5, "You must not bow down to them [idols] or worship them, for I, the Lord your God, am a jealous God who will not tolerate your affection for any other gods" (NLT). We are not to bow down—acknowledge allegiance to or worship of—anyone or anything other than the one true, all-powerful God.

Some people, however, do not understand or view their sex and sexuality as a gift from God. Those who defy and reject God's design regarding their sex and sexuality are bowing down to the fantasy male or female they created in their mind. They are worshiping an idol.

---

[6] "Does Psalm 95:6 mean we should always bow down when we worship God?" GotQuestions.org, accessed June 26, 2023, https://www.gotquestions.org/let-us-worship-and-bow-down.html.

DIVINE RE-CREATION

The fall of Adam and Eve in Eden introduced imperfection into God's perfect world. People tempted by the fleshly desires of homosexuality and transgenderism are no different than Adam and Eve being tempted by their desire to reject their dependence on God and live independent of His Word. Romans 1:25 says, "They exchanged the truth about God for a lie and worshiped and served the creature rather than the Creator" (ESV). If we believe our identity comes from within us—the way we think or feel—we have exchanged truth for a lie. We have elevated the creature above the Creator.

The prophet Jeremiah wrote, "The heart is deceitful above all things, and desperately sick; who can understand it?" (Jeremiah 17:9 ESV). Only God can. We cannot plumb the depths of our heart or the deceptions it willingly embraces as truth. But through Jesus Christ, God can re-create us: "And I will give you a new heart, and a new spirit I will put within you. And I will remove the heart of stone from your flesh and give you a heart of flesh" (Ezekiel 36:26 ESV).

When we are left to our own devices, our stony hearts may be unwilling to hear God, which leads to an unwillingness to listen to His voice and to live according to His design. Praise God, though, for the work of the Holy Spirit, who penetrates our stony heart and creates a hunger to know God and obey His Word. This hunger opens the door to understanding who He designed us to be and a desire to lean into Him to become the awesome man or woman He created us to be.

CHAPTER TWO

REBELLION

When someone believes God made an error in the creation of man and woman, that person's heart and soul become darkened to God's truth. If he or she believes the devil's lie that God made this sort of error, where does the questioning of God's sovereignty and infallibility end?

For argument's sake, suppose I had believed the lie that I should have been a boy, which the serpent whispered to me in my younger years. What would the serpent have stolen from me? He would have taken the precious female life God gave me in exchange for a fantasy persona and a load of cultural deceptions like preferred pronouns: he, him, his, or maybe they, them, theirs. Once I embraced those lies, I would have moved from speaking lies to living lies.

If God made a mistake and I should have been a boy, I might have destroyed the healthy body parts He gave me by agreeing to have surgical procedures and hormone injections. More than likely, I would have taken anxiety and anti-depression medication for the remainder of my life so I could continue to live the lie. Furthermore, I would have cast aside respect for God as the higher authority, because I would have crowned myself the higher authority.

THE CONSEQUENCES OF REBELLION

Every sin has a ripple effect, and the attempt to become one's own God wreaks havoc on those who love the rebel dearly. In fact, when family members and friends discard their biblical viewpoints and support the rebel's deceptions, the rebel's sin is extended to others—luring them into deception and into disobedience to God.

Scripture equates rebellion with witchcraft. Through the prophet Samuel, God said to King Saul, "For rebellion is as the sin of witchcraft, and stubbornness is as iniquity and idolatry" (1 Samuel 15:23 NKJV). Witchcraft usually involves the worship of Satan and his demons; rebellion is often the worship of self. Both sins rob God of the glory and honor He deserves as Creator.

Rebellion also makes God angry. Jesus didn't die for our sins so we can live in rebellion and spit on God's grace. The "but we're all sinners" excuse does not justify living in darkness. God expects all His children to live in the light: "For at one time you were darkness, but now you are light in the Lord. Walk as children of light" (Ephesians 5:8 ESV).

Rebellion motivates a person to challenge authority and break rules. The Israelites rebelled against God in the wilderness, which is generally where a rebellious spirit leads us to—a barren, life-draining place. Psalm 78 is a plea for the writer's generation to avoid the mistakes their ancestors made. The psalmist pleads with his listeners to "set their hope in God and not forget the works of God, but keep his commandments; and that they should not be like their fathers, a stubborn and rebellious generation, a generation whose heart was not steadfast, whose spirit was not faithful to God" (vv. 7–8 ESV).

When someone exchanges his or her identity as male or female for a counterfeit label and life as transgender (trans, transvestite, cross-dresser) or uses opposite-sex pronouns that dishonor God as Creator, that person is living in rebellion. Devoted to their sinful lifestyle, they refuse to accept God's calling, relying on self rather than trusting in the Lord. The rebel is fleeing from the One who loves them the most, the only One who can provide the satisfaction and fulfillment that person craves.

Here's the sort of damage rebels do to themselves and their loved ones:

> Susan says, "I know transitioning isn't a God thing to do. But it's what I want to do for me. I figure they'll [family] get used to the idea at some point in their life if I persist. If they don't, that's on them."
>
> Samuel says, "I realize my womanhood goes against God, but I don't care."

When people like Susan and Samuel acknowledge what they are about to do goes against God's design and will but pursue it anyway, sin has control of their spirit. The same is true for someone who confesses he or she doesn't care what God or parents or other loved ones say. Again, that person has set himself or herself up as god, and that is rebellion.

Here are some insightful thoughts about rebellion:

> The Old Testament used the Hebrew word *meri* that translates to the English word *rebellion*. The root of this Hebrew word, *mara*, means "to be or cause to be

bitter or unpleasant." It is also translated most often as change, disobedient, disobey, provoke, rebellious, and rebel.

In the New Testament, similar words for rebellion are disobedience and sedition, both of which refer to rebelling against or undermining authority. Interestingly, the Greek word for disobedience comes from the same root for the word disbelief as described in an obstinate or rebellious way.[7]

Rebellion against God is defiance of or disobedience against His authority. In disobedience, people tell God to get out of their way so they can live the way they want to live, sadly without Him. This allows their heart to become calloused and, if unchecked, leads to embracing and excusing rebellion against God. As rebellion darkens the heart, the person commits more sin.

God will not tolerate the rebellion. There will be consequences.

GOD-GIVEN DOMINION

In Genesis 1:26–28, God gave Adam dominion over every living thing on the earth:

> Then God said, "Let us make mankind in our image, in our likeness, so that they may rule over the fish in the sea and the birds in the sky, over the livestock and all

---

[7] Michael L. Williams, Dr., "What Does the Bible Say about Rebellion? A Christian Study," What Christians Want to Know, accessed June 27, 2013, https://www.whatchristianswanttoknow.com/what-does-the-bible-say-about-rebellion-a-christian-study/#ixzz85NXirClq.

the wild animals, and over all the creatures that move along the ground. . . .

God blessed them and said to them, "Be fruitful and increase in number; fill the earth and subdue it. Rule over the fish in the sea and the birds in the sky and over every living creature that moves on the ground."

Note these words: *rule, subdue.* With this dominion comes authority and responsibility, which, sadly, may lead to rebellion against the One who provided the authority in the first place.

As people move toward rebellion, they reject the dominion God entrusted to them and choose instead to do the opposite of His instructions and will, which leads to an ever-widening, more life-threatening quicksand pit of sin. The prophet Isaiah identified a progression of sinful behaviors connected to rebellion: "For our offenses are many in your sight, and our sins testify against us. Our offenses are ever with us, and we acknowledge our iniquities: rebellion and treachery against the LORD, turning our backs on God, inciting revolt and oppression, uttering lies our hearts have conceived" (Isaiah 59:12–13). In verses 14–15, he notes the outcome of these behaviors: "So justice is driven back, and righteousness stands at a distance; truth has stumbled in the streets, honesty cannot enter. Truth is nowhere to be found and whoever shuns evil becomes a prey."

First Corinthians 14:33 reminds us that "God is not a God of disorder but of peace." Within His church and among His people, He desires that everything be done "in a fitting and orderly way" (1 Corinthians 14:40). When we respect authority and exercise proper dominion, we can care for other people and all of God's creation the way He wants us to care for them. Doing this also models what God does for us, which sets the stage to protect and care for those who are most vulnerable in our society.

Satan will attempt to deceive and discourage those who are vulnerable and gullible. He will use misconceptions to draw a person closer to him and further away from God's perfect design and will. Satan whispers lies about circumstances, and he is quite good at convincing people their feelings or beliefs are the right way to keep their life in perfect harmony as he waits for them to walk in complete rebellion.

Those who claim to seek justice drive it further away by rebelling against God and embracing lies. Those who claim to seek equality destroy it by oppressing those who disagree with them. When we allow Satan to twist our God-given dominion into rebellion, we will move farther and farther away from what we most desire—fulfillment, purpose, well-being.

ANGER AND REBELLION

Sometimes we may be under the authority of a boss or someone else who is not kind and loving. This type of situation understandably makes us angry. However, another person's wrongdoing does not change the fact that as Christians we are called to respect and submit to another's authority as long as we are not required to violate Scripture. Romans 12 provides some guidelines for these situations:

- Be joyful in hope, patient in affliction, faithful in prayer (v. 12).

- Bless those who persecute you; bless and do not curse (v. 14).
- Live in harmony with one another (v. 16).
- Do not repay evil for evil (v. 17).
- If it is possible, as far as it depends on you, live at peace with everyone (v. 18).

How is it possible to put this teaching into practice? The key is given in verse 12: be faithful in prayer. Ask God to help you see the difficult authority figure from His perspective. He loves that person and may be calling you to let His love for that individual flow through you.

In the end, doing what is right by God's Word pleases Him, and He will set things right in accordance with His eternal plan. Romans 12:19 says, "Do not take revenge, my dear friends, but leave room for God's wrath, for it is written: 'It is mine to avenge; I will repay,' says the Lord." Trust God to administer justice in His time in His way. And though we may not see why, His way is often "do not be overcome by evil, but overcome evil with good" (Romans 12:21).

A sense of injustice may lead us to anger, which in turn may lead to rebellion. When you feel that first twinge of injustice, take it to God. Ask Him to fill you with gratitude and trust and praise instead—time-tested preventives for rebellion.

CHOOSE REPENTANCE

Rebellion has existed ever since the archangel Lucifer said, "I will ascend to the heavens; I will raise my throne above the stars of God; I will sit enthroned on the mount of assembly; . . .

I will ascend above the tops of the clouds; I will make myself like the Most High" (Isaiah 14:13–14 NIV).

He has been inciting rebellion ever since. Nothing gives him more pleasure than seeing human beings follow his path to destruction via rebellion against their Creator. That disastrous journey often begins with the thought that God has made a mistake or has been unfair.

Don't yield to the lie that rebellion is a path to independence, happiness, satisfaction, or fulfillment. It will only lead to unhappiness and disappointment. Through the prophet Hosea, God gave this promise to those who repent: "I will heal their waywardness and love them freely" (Hosea 14:4). Hosea then added his own plea for repentance: "Who is wise? Let them realize these things. Who is discerning? Let them understand. The ways of the LORD are right; the righteous walk in them, but the rebellious stumble in them" (v. 9).

Our earnest prayer should be that God changes our heart as we allow Him to mold us into the people He designed us to be and yield to His plans for our lives. Perhaps a fitting prayer is, "Change my heart, oh God."

CHAPTER THREE

ENVY

Eric confessed to me his dislike for being male and his envy of all females. He was resentful that he had not been given the attention his younger sister received every time she sat on their stepdad's lap. As Eric unwrapped his story, he shared the emotional high he experienced when male road workers whistled at him as he passed, dressed as a woman. The excitement filled his empty emotional bank. He felt worthy and valuable. He admitted, "I received the attention I've needed for so long."

Eric also spoke of his broken marriages and his current relationship struggles with a biological man whose mother does not know Eric was born male. His mother-in-law is so kind to him, he said, and his "husband's" family loves him.

Eric experienced so little love growing up. He left home at age seventeen, and now in his early thirties, he admits he has never been back home, even though he sometimes misses his mom. He also realizes how his damaging home environment and his envy toward his sister drove him to his willful actions. But he confesses he doesn't know the way out of the prison of lust that drove him to become Elaine.

ENVY'S DELUSION

Envy is a root sin that needs to be confronted and eradicated when unlocking the mystery and confusion of people who want to become someone other than the person God ordained and created them to be. Envy nourishes a person's lust and will never be satisfied until the person is consumed by fantasies, self-destructive behavior, and excruciating emotional pain. Ultimately, the person loses touch with reality. His or her relationship with God is also at risk. Eric said, "Reality is not part of my life. I pretend every day to be someone I really am not."

Envy can give a person the illusion of power, of control. As I mentioned in chapter two, Satan was envious of God and wanted to usurp His power (Isaiah 14:13–14). But Satan's current power is a fantasy. He still answers to God, as the book of Job indicates (1:6–2:8), and one day God will cast Satan into "the lake of fire and sulfur," where he "will be tormented day and night forever and ever" (Revelation 20:10 ESV).

Envy never delivers what it promises.

Instead, it actually weakens us at our core. Proverbs 14:30 says, "A heart at peace gives life to the body, but envy rots the bones." Envy causes us to be always running but never finding rest. Solomon, who was wiser than any other human being, warned, "And I saw that all toil and all achievement spring from one person's envy of another. This too is meaningless, a chasing after the wind "(Ecclesiastes 4:4).

Eric spent years seeing himself as less valuable and unlovable. He invested hundreds of hours in negatively comparing his maleness with the female attributes he thought he needed to make him feel loved and equal to his sister. His strong jealousy of his sister consumed him so much that he attempted to become his version of her. The lie he believed became the prison cell he volunteered to live in and continues to inhabit.

Envy wreaks havoc as long a person allows it to rule his or her life.

PATHWAY TO DESTRUCTION

Envy can take hold of anyone's life, just as it did with Eric. And once envy has a grip on your life, other sins are likely to follow it and to feed it, leaving you in chaos as you follow its path toward destruction.

James says, "For where you have envy and selfish ambition, there you find disorder and every evil practice" (James 3:16). Peter urges Christians to "rid yourselves of all malice and all deceit, hypocrisy, envy, and slander of every kind" (1 Peter 2:1). Paul lists various "acts of the flesh," with "envy" listed alongside "idolatry" and "fits of rage." He adds that "those who live like this will not inherit the kingdom of God" (Galatians 5:19–21).

According to *Easton's Bible Dictionary*, idolatry is "image-worship or divine honour paid to any created object."[8] The apostle Paul explains the origin of idolatry in Romans 1:21–25:

> For although they knew God, they neither glorified him as God nor gave thanks to him, but their thinking became futile and their foolish hearts were darkened. Although they claimed to be wise, they became fools and exchanged the glory of the immortal God for images made to look like a mortal human being and

---

[8] "Idolatry," Easton's Bible Dictionary, BibleStudyTools.com, accessed July 10, 2023, https://www.biblestudytools.com/dictionary/idolatry/.

> birds and animals and reptiles. Therefore God gave them over in the sinful desires of their hearts to sexual impurity for the degrading of their bodies with one another. They exchanged the truth about God for a lie, and worshiped and served created things rather than the Creator—who is forever praised. Amen.

When a man or woman allows envy or lust to lead them off the path God has for them, consequences, similar to those Eric is experiencing, will surely follow. Unfortunately, sometimes those consequences last a lifetime. Consider what Scott Newgent, a transman, shared at the 2023 What Is a Woman? Conference:

> I'm here to end the idea that medically transitioning children is about human rights. It is not. It's about money. Market research predicts that gender-affirming care will generate more than 5 billion dollars a year in less than a decade. . . . The truth is that medical transition is experimental, dangerous, and it doesn't cure anything.
>
> I underwent close to one million dollars' worth of surgeries and hormone therapies to change from Kelly to Scott, a transman, and I almost died in the process. And I've certainly cut many years off my life. In fact, I probably won't live long enough to meet my grandkids because I still to this day get reoccurring infections. Nobody knows why. But again, 95% of all medical transition is experimental.
>
> I tried to kill off my female self. I was told a lie. I was told that I was a man trapped in a woman's body, that

my masculine traits and my strong personality were proof that I was really a man. I was told that all my pain and self-loathing would magically disappear if only I pumped my body with testosterone, removed my breasts, and altered my genitalia. I was tricked at 42 at a vulnerable place.[9]

Satan is the master of finding our vulnerable place and exploiting it. The apostle Peter reminds us that Satan is out to "devour" us (1 Peter 5:8). He may begin with an emotion as seemingly harmless as admiration. But he knows how easy it is for admiration to become desire, then envy, then lust. All of them lead to destruction.

THE LIE OF GREENER GRASS

The consequences of envy are great. The false belief that the "grass is greener on the other side" is misleading and dangerous to the soul, heart, and body. Buying into the lie of greener pastures is older than Eden. It originated with Satan. The prophet Ezekiel reveals that Lucifer was "the seal of perfection, full of wisdom and perfect in beauty. . . . you were blameless in your ways from the day you were created till wickedness was found in you" (Ezekiel 28: 12, 15).

If it could happen to a being as magnificent as Lucifer, it can certainly happen to any one of us.

---

[9] Scott Newgent, viewed on Facebook page of John Zigomanis, July 10, 2023, https://www.facebook.com/100008332983099/posts/1435212550348995/?vh=e&extid=MSG-UNK-UNK-UNK-IOS_GK0T-GK1C.

Raymond B. Egan and Richard A. Whiting published "The Grass Is Always Greener (in the Other Fellow's Yard)" in 1924. The song's lyrics emphasize how human it is to view what someone else has as better than what we have.[10] For some people, the prospect of a different body, home, husband, or children may appear to be greener grass. But the truth is, no matter which side of the lawn we view, every lawn has crabgrass and weeds—maybe even destructive slugs and moles underneath the surface.

A WINNABLE WAR

Most of the time, the smiles plastered on our faces only reveal how well we can hide the truth about our lives. But the grass is equally green on both sides if we allow God to help us see ourselves as He does. What David said about himself in Psalm 139 is true of us all: "Body and soul, I am marvelously made!" (v. 14, MSG). The word *marvelous* means "fundamentally exceptional in character or quality; being or having the characteristics of a miracle; of the highest kind or quality."[11] When we accept God's view of us, Satan loses his grip on our life.

Those who struggle with gender confusion are living under a deception they've not yet detected. Perhaps it is hidden under their emotional pain and the lies they've believed about who God really is.

God is not the one who tempts anyone to envy or lust. He does not lead anyone toward the desire to mutilate their body or to

---

[10] Listen to the song on YouTube, https://www.youtube.com/watch?v=8ih-kt96CgA.

[11] "Marvelous," Merriam-Webster Online Dictionary, accessed July 10, 2023, https://unabridged.merriam-webster.com/unabridged/marvelous.

live under the assumption they are the opposite gender. James gives us this counsel:

> Let no one say when he is tempted, "I am tempted from God" [for temptation does not originate from God, but from our own flaws]; for God cannot be tempted by [what is] evil, and He Himself tempts no one. But each one is tempted when he is dragged away, enticed and baited [to commit sin] by his own [worldly] desire [lust, passion]. Then when the illicit desire has conceived, it gives birth to sin; and when sin has run its course, it gives birth to death. (James 1:13–16 AMP)

The apostle Peter reminds us that Satan is the one who "prowls around like a roaring lion, seeking someone to devour" (1 Peter 5:8 ESV). Satan, not God, can fill a mind with urges and desires that seem too powerful to resist. Over the years, I've talked to many people who have expressed that the fight against compulsions to cross-dress, or to live in the fantasy of being someone other than they are, can seem unwinnable. But that, too, is Satan's lie. This war is winnable. The Bible tells us, "God blesses those who patiently endure testing and temptation" (James 1:12 NLT).

When you wake up in the morning and feel envy rising inside you or feel the tug of wanting to become someone else, remind yourself that envy is a form of unbelief that leads you away from God's true goodness. Get your Bible out, kneel before God, ask Him to pour out His guidance and wisdom on you. Keep praying and keep reading your Bible until envy flees.

Lastly, ask God to surround you with His peace and love. Ask Him to help you accept His reality of who you are. The truth will change your life if you truly desire and want it to.

CHAPTER FOUR

MANIPULATION

One of Satan's favorite tools is manipulation—twisting facts to deceive people and to serve his own diabolical purposes. He used it in Eden with Adam and Eve. Later, he used it in an attempt to destroy Sarai's (later called Sarah) and Abram's (later called Abraham) relationship with God.

Here's how biblical counselor June Hunt describes what happened to this couple that God had chosen as the father and mother of the nation of Israel:

> The couple sets off for Egypt to escape a famine, but before setting foot into the foreign land, Abram decides to "fabricate" a tale, twisting the truth. This first patriarch of the faith fears for his life because if the Egyptians discover he is married to beautiful Sarai, they might kill him in order to take her into Pharaoh's harem.[12]

So Abram says to Sarai, "I know what a beautiful woman you are. . . . Say you are my sister, so that I will be treated well for your sake and my life will be spared because of you" (Genesis 12:11–13). Sarai agrees to go along with the story.

---

[12] June Hunt, *Manipulation* (Torrence, CA: Rose Publishing, 2013), 10.

"Bottom line," writes Hunt, "Abram manipulates the facts."[13] Sarai is his half-sister but also his wife (Genesis 20:12). Therefore, instead of trusting God and relying on His faithfulness to do what He had promised, Abram and Sarai begin a cycle of manipulative behavior that lasts many decades.

Hunt defines manipulation as "the art of controlling people or circumstances by indirect, unfair, or deceptive means—especially to one's own advantage." She adds that "manipulation happens to those who allow others to have excessive control over them—the control that God alone should have."[14]

Satan loves to deceive us into believing that we are in control when actually he is controlling us. He is a master of gaining control of people through manipulative tactics and also encouraging people to manipulate one another for self-serving purposes. How better to serve self than to pretend to be your own creator and defy God's authority and design?

THE TRANSGENDER LIE

No one can truly recreate their human body. As I pointed out in chapter one, genetic research indicates male and female markers are present in our DNA. People can take opposite-sex hormones, and they can alter their outward appearance, but they cannot change what makes them biologically male or female.

In 1917, Alberta Lucille Hart (aka Alan L. Hart) was one of the first people to undergo what now falls under the category

---

[13] Hunt, 10.

[14] Hunt, 10.

of gender-affirming surgery.[15] In the following decades, a small percentage of other people pursued surgeries that changed their appearance from male-to-female or female-to-male.

But even ten years ago, no one would have imagined the number of people who now choose to remove healthy body parts in order to create the illusion of another person—one of their own making. In March 2021, a Current Urology case report estimated that "there are about 9,000 transgender surgeries being performed annually across the United States."[16] Sadly, these life-altering surgeries are not only performed on adults but also on children and teens, even though the long-term health risks for these surgeries are unknown. In spite of the fact that US government, education, and medical authorities continue to push LGBTQ ideology, the National Library of Medicine recently revealed that "individuals who underwent gender-affirming surgery had a 12.12-fold higher suicide attempt risk than those who did not."[17]

---

[15] "Gender-Affirming Surgery," Wikipedia, accessed August 4, 2023, https://en.wikipedia.org/wiki/Gender-affirming_surgery.

[16] Vishnu R. Mani, Sebastian C. Valdevieso, et al., "Transgender Surgery—Knowledge Gap Among Physicians Impacting Patient Care," Current Urology, March 2021, https://journals.lww.com/cur/fulltext/2021/03000/transgender_surgery___knowledge_gap_among.12.aspx#:~:text=There%20are%20about%209000%20transgender,result%20in%20gender%2Daffirming%20surgeries.

[17] John J. Straub, Krishna K. Paul, Lauren G. Bothwell, et al. "Risk of Suicide and Self-Harm Following Gender-Affirmation Surgery," National Library of Medicine, April 16, 2024, https://www.ncbi.nlm.nih.gov/pmc/articles/PMC11063965/.

Some European countries have stopped approving these surgeries for pre-pubescent boys and girls.[18] In April 2024, UK pediatrician Dr. Hilary Cass released a study showing that "children have been let down by a lack of research and 'remarkably weak' evidence" that "medical interventions in gender care" are in their best interest. The National Health Service in England also announced that "hormones that 'stop the progress of puberty'— would no longer be routinely prescribed, and should only be given to gender-distressed children as part of clinical trials."[19]

The idea of creating a living person out of body parts can be traced back to Mary Shelley's nineteenth-century novel *Frankenstein*. The book is "simultaneously the first sciencefiction novel, a Gothic horror, a tragic romance and a parable all sewn into one towering body. . . . Its two central tragedies—one of overreaching and the dangers of 'playing God,' the other of parental abandonment and societal rejection—are as relevant today as ever."[20] In the novel, Dr. Frankenstein decides to play God and create life. Once the creature is given life, however, the doctor abhors the monster he created and seeks to destroy it. He never even gives it a name.

In the twenty-first century, medical advancements have given doctors the ability to fabricate life—not new life but different

---

[18] Leor Sapir, "Second Thoughts on 'Gender-Affirming Care,'" Wall Street Journal online, August 6, 2023, https://www.wsj.com/articles/second-thoughts-on-gender-affirming-care-american-academy-pediatrics-doctors-review-medicine-a7173276?mod=opinion_lead_pos9.

[19] Josh Parry, "Hilary Cass: Weak Evidence Letting Children Down over Gender Care," April 10, 2024, British Broadcasting Company (BBC), https://www.bbc.com/news/health-68770641.

[20] Rebecca Laurence, "Why Frankenstein Is the Story That Defines Our Fears," BBC, June 13, 2018, https://www.bbc.com/culture/article/20180611-why-frankenstein-is-the-story-that-defined-our-fears.

life. They can take a living person and change his or her appearance through hormonal treatments and surgical procedures. Physicians, pharmaceutical companies, mental health workers, and others are engaging in god-like behavior without any consideration of, or deference to, the One who designed the human body in the first place. These professionals manipulate vulnerable individuals by creating a false belief. Their actions demonstrate a defiance of God as Creator. No human being can create life out of nothing; only God can do that.

By misleading vulnerable people and manipulating reality, these medical and corporate professionals have generated destructive conflicts within many families, and cultural pressure to embrace this false reality has reached an all-time high. I heard one person say, "Let's call it [transgenders] the community." After all, the word *community* sounds peaceful, nurturing, and normal. But the massive increase in younger people identifying under the LGBTQ banner is anything but normal:

> "Since Fall 2010, Brown [University]'s LGBTQ+ population has expanded considerably. The gay or lesbian population has increased by 26% and the percentage of students identifying as bisexual has increased by 232%," the student newspaper reported. "Students identifying as other sexual orientations within the LGBTQ+ community have increased by 793%."[21]

---

[21] Matt Lamb, "Forty Percent of Brown University Students Say They Are LGBT, Suggesting Social Contagion," in the Washington Examiner, accessed September 14, 2024. https://www.washingtonexaminer.com/opinion/beltway-confidential/2787746/forty-percent-of-brown-university-students-say-they-are-lgbt-suggesting-social-contagion-2/.

As we witness such a swift change in how younger generations view or identify themselves, it's easy to see how a social contagion spreads, but don't think for a minute academics will acknowledge it. After all, if they did admit such a contagion is possible, they'd be facing the reality that gayness and transgenderism are not innate. They would have to concede and confess to the manipulative spirit of peer pressure and delusion they use.

MANIPULATIVE AUTHORITY FIGURES

In John 8:44 Jesus says to the religious leaders, "You are of your father the devil, and your will is to do your father's desires. He was a murderer from the beginning, and does not stand in the truth, because there is no truth in him. When he lies, he speaks out of his own character, for he is a liar and the father of lies" (ESV).

In his great war against God, Satan will go down with his very last breath trying to steal what God has given to every human—a body, mind, and spirit created in the image of God. For Satan, no one is off limits, including children. They are the ideal candidates for his deception because of their vulnerability and impressionability. He also uses children because adults, who may be willing to take a stand against him in some circumstances, will yield to his pressure when a child is involved.

After all, no one wants to see a child suffer, and if a child "can't help" his confusion about his biological sex or manage his conflicting emotions, then that child must have been born in the wrong body, right? This exaltation of a child's feelings above all common sense is rebellion against God, the Creator. No child (or adult for that matter) has the right to say to God, "You have made a mistake. My feelings tell me I am the opposite sex, so that is what I am."

Indeed, Satan rolls out the red carpet for these children by manipulating hundreds of caring adults who are "safeguarding" children's rights and health care. School administrators, faculty, and board members champion the cultish practice of separating children from the influence of their parents:

> Nova High School and Meany Middle School offer on-site health services including both medical and counseling services through Country Doctor Community Health Centers (CDCHC), a local non-profit that also runs two primary care clinics, according to the schools' websites. While the school websites do not specify what "gender affirming" services they offer in their clinics, the CDCHC offers cross-sex hormones, referrals for cross-sex surgeries and help with obtaining letters of support for those seeking such procedures, according to their website.[22]

> Though school districts for years have gone behind the backs of parents to ensure their agenda goes through, it gets even worse beginning with Governor Gavin Newsom in California. He "signed a bill last night [September 29, 2022] empowering state courts to remove out-of-state children from their parent's custody if those children come to California because they can't get sterilizing transgender drugs and mutilating surgeries

---

[22] Laurel Duggan, "Seattle Public Schools Offer 'Gender Affirming Care,' Hide Transgender Status from Parents," Daily Caller, July 11, 2023, https://dailycaller.com/2023/07/11/seattle-public-schools-offer-gender-affirming-care-hide-transgender-status-from-parents/?pnespid=rLZlAycaKL8C3KGR_S2mCIuGpxirT4duNfLtkLZ38BRmX.UtLjQtdSFf_iL1Hdv_dQ85d.s9jQ.

in their home states or because their parents object to these experimental treatments for gender dysphoria."[23]

If you think parents still have rights over their children's mental and physical well-being, think again. Our culture tells us that the time has come to accept the idea Hillary Clinton promoted way back in 1996: "It takes all of us. Yes, it takes a village."[24] But who is in charge of the so-called village? It sure isn't the parents; rather, it's the people who live to deconstruct society and any moral standards God desires us to live by.

Hospitals join in the push to destroy the mental and physical health of the most vulnerable ones, our children, those who most need our protection:

> Seattle Children's Hospital offers education guides that encourage medical professionals to quickly offer cross-sex medical treatments such as menstrual suppression and puberty blockers to youth patients with gender identity issues. The guides largely fail to mention mental health services, and indicate that they are optional and must be sought through outside institutions; the hospital's gender clinic does not offer long-term mental health therapy.[25]

---

[23] Greg Burt, "Gov. Newsome Signs Bill to Strip Children from Parents to Medically Transgender Them," California Family Council, September 30, 2022, https://www.californiafamily.org/2022/09/gov-newsom-signs-bill-to-strip-children-from-parents-to-medically-transgender-them/.

[24] Hillary Clinton, "It Takes a Village," DNC address delivered August 27, 1996, Chicago, Illinois, American Rhetoric, accessed July 31, 2023, https://www.americanrhetoric.com/speeches/hillaryclintontakesavillage.htm

[25] Megan Brock and Laurel Duggan, "'Appalling: Unearthed Documents Reveal How Hospital Pushes Medical Transitions on Children," Daily Caller, April 27, 2023, https://dailycaller.com/2023/04/27/seattle-childrens-gender-transitions/?pnespid=7_

These are the empowering agencies (school authorities, government officials, and medical professionals) whom we are told have our children's best interest at heart. But they do not.

SPEAK THE TRUTH

Misleading others by presenting lies as truth is a dangerous form of manipulation. Thousands of people have been manipulated to believe that hormone treatments, surgical procedures, ongoing therapy, anti-depressants, anxiety medications, and dilators for a man-made cervix are prescribed in the name of love. If this is love, I sure don't know what hate is. The desire to somehow usurp God's throne of authority and His sovereign power to create life is wicked—a wickedness Satan knows all too well.

In a 2023 hearing before Congress, detransitioner Chloe Cole said, "I didn't need to be lied to. I needed compassion. I needed to be loved. I need to be getting therapy to help me work through my issues."[26] She also said that "the gender specialist" she was taken to gave her parents an ultimatum: "'Would you rather have a dead daughter or a living transgender son?'"[27]

This manipulative either-or scenario is used repeatedly by medical professionals, LGBTQ activists, and gender-confused individuals to pressure others to "do as I say or else . . ." Yet even Sweden's study on long-term follow-up of transsexual persons who have undergone sex reassignment surgery found

---

ZqEC5Yaaoe1vSZ9mjlHYuLuwr1SJwmduS22bRsthNmYH2OOf_.O2wghokist3PsWtLdSwfHg.

[26] Chloe Cole, "'My Childhood Was Ruined': Detransitioner Chloe Cole Talks about Trans Procedures," YouTube, accessed July 27, 2023, https://www.youtube.com/watch?v=DSGgR3W_jjg.

[27] Cole, "My Childhood Was Ruined."

that "persons with transsexualism, after sex reassignment, have considerably higher risks for mortality, suicidal behaviour, and psychiatric morbidity than the general population. [Their] findings suggest that sex reassignment, although alleviating gender dysphoria, may not suffice as treatment for transsexualism, and should inspire improved psychiatric and somatic care after sex reassignment for this patient group."[28]

This study actually presents the truth. Yet the US government along with education and medical professionals are using scare tactics to cause us and our loved ones to live in fear because of the lies about gender they've told so many times through the years.

It's past time to stand up against these powerful agencies by using the power of speaking truth over and over again just as they've repeatedly manipulated thousands of people with their lies. We must be brave and go forth to battle at whatever level God asks of us. For some of us, it may be running for a local or county government office; it may be pursuing a leadership position on a local school board. God may want us to speak at a state or federal Senate or House hearing. He may ask us to begin a prayer group that meets regularly with those concerned and willing to go to battle on their knees for God's intervention in the midst of the evil we face.

Every parent or caregiver can begin to teach children about these issues at an age-appropriate level. Give the facts about their birth. Tell them about God's design and purpose for every

---

[28] Cecilia Dhejne, Paul Lichtenstein, Marcus Boman, Anna L. V. Johansson, et al., "Long-term Follow-up of Transsexual Persons Undergoing Sex Reassignment Surgery: Cohort Study in Sweden," NIH: National Library of Medicine, accessed July 23, 2023, https://pubmed.ncbi.nlm.nih.gov/21364939/.

person. Bring them into conversations by asking, "What do you think?" Listen to their viewpoint, but always point them toward the Word of God for answers about gender identity and healthy self-image.

STAND AGAINST MANIPULATIVE TACTICS

Those in the LGBTQ community often use manipulation against their own relatives. Family members are scared that if they don't do what the manipulator is pressuring them do, they will:

- Lose a relationship with them.
- Lose a false power they feel they have to change their loved one's ways.
- Lose them to suicide which, of course, is the greatest concern.

I wonder if the LGBTQ loved one has any idea that they are not controlling anyone, but rather they are allowing Satan to control them by using the Father of Lies' misleading and manipulative tactics.

My father operated out of a manipulative spirit to attempt to get what he wanted many times. He was completely focused on what his inner self was leading him to do to control me and others to give him the results he sought after.

For instance, a letter he wrote to my mother gave her four stipulations if he were to return home:

> I have been thinking about the things that would need to take place if I came home. We need to agree to this in order to not go into this blindly:

First, how the neighbors will react to our family?

Second, how long will you allow me to shave my body?

Thirdly, how often and for how long I will wear women's nightgowns?

Fourth, to recognize I will be wearing woman's panties for the rest of my life.

Fifth, shall I pack my clothes and we see if things will work out?

These things may not seem important to you, but they are to me. The kids would have to deal with these and maybe more things.

God Bless you,

Harold C. German, Dad

With all my love

PS. No letter from Denise yet.

Thankfully, my mom did not allow the manipulative spirit he was living under rule her. She did not agree to his rules. If she had, it would have only destroyed her at another level, living under the roof day in and day out under this ruining, destructive satanic spirit.

RESPOND IN LOVE AND TRUTH

My dad never wanted to face truth or be responsible. But it is truth that sets a person free (John 8:32). We have choices to make. We can agree with the lies someone believes for the sake of avoiding pain. We can agree to abide by someone else's rules and live in fear, lips gagged. Or we can choose to live by the truth.

Begin conversations with statements like these:

> "I'm sorry you don't understand why I can't call you by ___. But I cannot say what does not reflect my heart."

> "I understand you feel this way, but feelings do change."

A simple testimony of what you've been through in life and how God met you where you were, or where you are, can be a testimony of hope to someone entering your home or church. Stories are a powerful way to share about how God has demonstrated His greatness and love in your life. But be on guard: Satan's manipulative spirit may continue to hold control over the other person and may use other methods to control you. You need to be vigilant and let the person know you are aware of the new technique being used in an attempt to control you. Encourage the person to focus on the Lord to meet their unmet needs.

As God's people, we grow in faith and courage when we keep our eyes on Him. We must be careful to not make the mistake of keeping our eyes on our loved one, of making them our idol, of setting them up as our all and all-for. That kind of mindset places the loved one on God's throne in our lives. Galatians 1:10 speaks powerfully about this: "Am I now trying to win the approval of human beings, or of God? Or am I trying to please people? If I were trying to please people, I would not be a servant of Christ."

You can take control of how you're handling a manipulator. You don't have to allow the person (or organization) to control you. It's not your Christian duty to take the abuse of false accusations, lies, belittlement, or any other kind of spiritual, mental, or physical abuse that a manipulator inflicts on you. Rather, it is your duty to remain faithful to God. His truths and His ways should be your primary concern. Focus on pleasing God, not people.

I began this chapter with the story of Abram and Sarai's behavior in Egypt. Their cycle of manipulation and lies began when they doubted God's promise to keep them safe in the land He told them to live in. They yielded to fear and went to Egypt. Then they yielded to fear again and lied about their marital status. Sarai ended up in Pharaoh's harem, and God had to intervene (Genesis 12:14–20). Abram and Sarai left Egypt, but they did not leave their manipulative behavior there. The Bible records two more incidents when they resorted to manipulation in Genesis 16:1–16 and Genesis 20:1–18. Both times God intervened and held them accountable.

Manipulation is a subtle form of deceit and falsehood, but it is still sin. Proverbs 12:22 says, "Lying lips are an abomination to the Lord, but those who act faithfully are his delight" (ESV). God calls us to a higher standard. "Rather, speaking the truth in love, we are to grow up in every way into him who is the head, into Christ" (Ephesians 4:15 ESV).

We don't need to give in to the manipulative behavior of others; neither do we need to resort to manipulative behavior ourselves. Our truth-loving, wise God can show us how to stand firm in His ways and be loving at the same time.

CHAPTER FIVE

MINIMIZING SIN

Another way Satan gains power over us and our loved ones is through minimizing sin. He takes advantage of our human tendency to justify our thoughts, behaviors, and actions. I don't want to think of myself as a sinner, and Satan is eager to reinforce these kinds of thoughts in my head: "I'm a good person" and "I'm only human" and "I have no other choice" and "It makes me happy. How can it be wrong?"

He probably uses the same tactic on you.

As we become desensitized to sin, we fail to have the proper response toward it, whether it is our sin or sin in others. We minimize it, justify it, or simply ignore it and go on our way, thinking we are unaffected by it.

When it comes to relationships, we can minimize sin in numerous ways. For instance, I might say, "I don't want to hurt my daughter's feelings, so I won't say anything about her decision to take male hormone treatments." Or "I don't want to cause friction in the family, so I'll attend my nephew's same-sex wedding even though I believe it dishonors God." Those who struggle with gender identity may excuse their actions by saying, "It's only clothing. What's wrong with me dressing like a man (when a woman) or as a woman (when a man)?"

Any of us can justify any action and twist it to make sense in our mind. But does this make our behavior right? Does this mean God is okay with our sin? No. It only means we humans know how to justify our actions to attain the desired result with as little guilt as possible.

When I began digging into my Bible to see what God said about my dad wearing women's clothing, the Holy Spirit led me to this verse: "A woman must not wear men's clothing, nor a man wear women's clothing, for the LORD your God detests anyone who does this" (Deuteronomy 22:5 NIV). *Detests* is a strong word. Other Bible versions use *abomination* (ESV), *utterly repulsive* (AMP), and *abhorrent* (TLB). How could God be any clearer than that? God loathes cross-dressing and other similar behaviors. They are sinful.

When I read that verse, I knew in my heart that my dad's behavior was wrong. It wasn't a matter of me judging him and just thinking his behavior was wrong. His behavior was unacceptable to God. God never intended for men and women to pretend to be the other sex. And He never condones this behavior. He abhors it.

IDOLATROUS BEHAVIORS

In Deuteronomy 5:8–10, God gives clear instructions about idols: "You shall not make for yourself an image in the form of anything in heaven above or on the earth beneath or in the waters below. You shall not bow down to them or worship them; for I, the LORD your God, am a jealous God, punishing the children for the sin of the parents to the third and fourth generation of those who hate me, but showing love to a thousand generations of those who love me and keep my commandments."

The *Merriam-Webster Dictionary* gives two definitions of idolatry: (1) the worship of a physical object as a god, and (2) immoderate attachment or devotion to something.[29] Dressing in the opposite sex's clothing is a form of idolatry because cross-dressers are creating a false image of who they are and obsessing over it. They are setting aside the person God designed them to be and choosing a fantasy. The more time, money, and attention they devote to the false image, the more it becomes the idol they worship.

Some justify cross-dressing as a form of acting, a way to entertain. But this behavior often leads participants into other kinds of sin. Romans 13:13 says, "Let us behave decently, as in the daytime, not in carousing and drunkenness, not in sexual immorality and debauchery, not in dissension and jealousy." How often are drag shows and other cross-dressing events also full of obscene gestures, sexual innuendos, and drunkenness? These behaviors lead people away from God and His standards of godliness. Those who love God are to be focused on "whatever is true, whatever is noble, whatever is right, whatever is pure, whatever is lovely, whatever is admirable" (Philippians 4:8).

Let's be honest. What is true, noble, right, pure, lovely, and admirable about living out the fantasy of being someone God never intended us to be?

---

[29] "Idolatry," Merriam-Webster Online Collegiate Dictionary, accessed January 9, 2024, https://unabridged.merriam-webster.com/collegiate/idolatry.

GOOD INTENTIONS, BAD OUTCOMES

Christians may be afraid to speak up because we fear we'll be called judgmental or intolerant if we don't attend a gay marriage or accept a person's false identity. These accusations are designed to hurt and belittle those who oppose the LGBTQ viewpoint. The derogatory labels are hurled at us to make us question our conscience and lead us away from God's Word and His ways—to minimize sins He abhors.

This insulting name game, straight from Satan's bag of tricks, sometimes works. Sarah shares, "Susie asked me to call her Sammy. I told her no again and again. But I confess, I became worn down and finally decided that if this is all Susie wants and peace will come, it's worth it." What Sarah, Susie's mother, did not expect, was how troubled her heart and soul became as she participated in Susie's fantasy. By giving in to her daughter, Sarah went against her moral convictions, which led to more inner turmoil, not peace.

Another way sin can be minimized by family members with good intentions is explained by this parent: "My son wants me to call him by his female names and pronouns. It's only this one thing he is asking for." The deceptive "this one thing" game is another of Satan's favorite tricks. We justify our decision or action by convincing ourselves that we'll only do it once or only give in on this one issue. But one act of disobedience is still disobedience. This mindset minimizes the sin by excusing the action you may be considering—only this time.

What happens when we do this? We allow ourselves to agree with the spirit of darkness that's controlling the matter at hand.

And just as it's difficult to eat only one potato chip or one M&M, it's extremely difficult to stop at "only this time" or "this one thing." Once darkness has seeped into our heart, it spreads rapidly.

Friends and family members are hungry for their dear one to see God in a genuine way, but participating in the self-made illusion of their loved one's fantasy cannot bring peace because it dishonors God and His intentional creation.

Giving in to the requests of your LGBTQ loved one may provide an illusion of peace—the temporary absence of conflict. But as Sarah discovered with her daughter Susie, the inner turmoil that results when we go against what we know the Bible says about an issue troubles our soul and drives a wedge between us and God. He is the only source of inner peace—well-being of mind, soul, and spirit.

AN ATTACK ON GOD AND HIS INFALLIBLE WORD

When people label us judgmental, intolerant, or some kind of "-phobe," they are ultimately attacking God, not us. If our convictions are aligned with His Word, the conflict is with God and His Word.

One of the biggest conflicts in the church today is between those who believe the Bible is the inspired Word of God and those who believe it merely provides principles by which to live—principles that need to be adapted to culture. After all, they say, the content of the Bible was composed and compiled centuries ago. How can it be relevant now unless we adjust its teachings to fit our culture?

God addressed the inspiration, infallibility, and eternal relevance of His Word in His Word:

> Every word of God is flawless; he is a shield to those who take refuge in him. Do not add to his words, or he will rebuke you and prove you a liar. Proverbs 30:5–6

> Heaven and earth will pass away, but my words will never pass away. Matthew 24:35

> All Scripture is God-breathed and is useful for teaching, rebuking, correcting and training in righteousness. 2 Timothy 3:16

> For prophecy never had its origin in the human will, but prophets, though human, spoke from God as they were carried along by the Holy Spirit. 2 Peter 1:21

We should handle God's Word with extreme care. As the 2 Timothy passage says, God Himself breathed Scripture into existence. Human beings have no right to mess with it. We have no right to say, "Well, God certainly didn't mean this or that." Even worse, how can we human beings conclude, "God must have been wrong about that. Scientists say . . . or activists say . . ."

The Word of God is holy—set apart and sacred. It is different from any other book ever written because its author is eternal and infallible. Its content should remain the same as it was when written without excluding teachings or misrepresenting them in any way.

A final warning about tampering with God's Word is given in Revelation 22:18–19, "For I testify to everyone who hears the words of the prophecy of this book: If anyone adds to these things, God will add to him the plagues that are written in this book" (NKJV). Sadly, these instructions have been ignored out of our human need to justify our lust or other sinful actions.

"A half century ago, A. W. Tozer preached these words: 'This is the day of excusing sin instead of purging sin. An entire school of thought has developed justifying sin within the church and trying to prove that sin is perfectly normal, and therefore acceptable.'"[30] When men or women excuse their sinful acts and continue to live a lie, attempting to fabricate the results they're looking for, they become comfortable in their sin. They see themselves through the lenses of self-deception and believe their actions are approved by our holy, almighty Creator God.

Make no mistake: denying the infallibility and eternal relevance of God's Word will lead to minimizing sin in your life and in others' lives. Only when we have an accurate view of God's Word can we have an accurate view of sin.

SATISFY YOUR SOUL HUNGER

If we're honest, we're all hungry. We're starving for something to sustain us, to preserve our hope, to strengthen us through trials, to help us conquer sin. We're starving for what will nourish and energize us for the everyday fight between sin and faith. But what food do we need for this battle? Jesus tells us: "Man shall not live on bread alone, but on every word that comes from the mouth of God" (Matthew 4:4). God's Word is the only food that can satisfy, sustain, and strengthen us.

---

[30] Bill Muehlenberg, "When the Church Proudly Embraces Sin," Billmuehlenberg.com., May 16, 2010, https://billmuehlenberg.com/2010/05/16/when-the-church-proudly-embraces-sin/.

If we are not good stewards of our soul, we can easily become addicted to spiritual junk food that will steal the life God intended for us. Eating this unhealthy food will lead us into other bad habits: selfish gain, lustful thoughts and actions, godless obsessions, excessive consumption, and even a restless laziness. They may make us feel full, they may temporarily satisfy a starving soul, but eventually our soul craves nourishment only God can supply.

God desires so much more for us than any fantasy we fabricate:

> His divine power has given us everything we need for a godly life through our knowledge of him who called us by his own glory and goodness. Through these he has given us his very great and precious promises, so that through them you may participate in the divine nature, having escaped the corruption of the world caused by evil desires. (2 Peter 1:3–4)

Divine nature or destructive fantasies?

The choice is ours.

God wants us to enjoy increasingly greater fellowship and intimacy with Him by becoming like Him, by growing in godliness. We enjoy life more by being more like God. He is Life. He is Love. He is Peace. He is Satisfaction.

In order to be like God, we must escape "the corruption of the world caused by evil desires" (2 Peter 1:4). Our greatest obstacle to knowing God intimately and enjoying our relationship with Him is our own corrupt desires. A corrupt heart and soul leave us begging for more, still starving for something greater than self. God knows better, and He offers us better.

Sinful desires and behaviors lead to suffering. The devil lies in secret, plotting to steal our life, joy, hope, and faith. He is delighted when we minimize sin and allow sinful desires and behaviors to deceive us and control us.

Turn to God instead. Yield to His divine power. Let Him uproot all sinful desires and get rid of all sinful indulgences. Ask Him to open your eyes to every way you minimize sin in your life and in your loved one's life. Ask Him to give you clarity and courage to address every sin in a way that honors Him.

An accurate view of sin will lead you into a more accurate view of God as the One who wants what is best for you. As you grow closer to Him, you'll be better able to embrace all "his very great and precious promises" and "participate in the divine nature." And you'll be moving toward the life He longs for you to enjoy.

CHAPTER SIX

GOOD AND EVIL

According to some, the existence of evil proves that God doesn't exist. Their argument goes something like this:

1. If God exists, then God is omnipotent, omniscient, and morally perfect.
2. If God is omnipotent, then God has the power to eliminate all evil.
3. If God is omniscient, then God knows when evil exists.
4. If God is morally perfect, then God has the desire to eliminate all evil.
5. Evil exists.
6. If evil exists, then either God doesn't have the power to eliminate all evil, or doesn't know when evil exists, or doesn't have the desire to eliminate all evil.
7. Therefore, God doesn't exist.[31]

Embracing this atheistic philosophy and denying there is a God is becoming increasingly popular with the growing Woke movement and the belief that humans can be their own creator through hormone treatments and surgeries. Many that self-identify as atheists or live as a transgender person do not believe in God any longer, even if they came from Christian homes.

---

[31] "The Problem of Evil," Stanford Encyclopedia of Philosophy, accessed March 13, 2024, https://plato.stanford.edu/entries/ evil/#:~:text=If%20 God%20is%20morally%20perfect,%2C%20God%20doesn%27t%20exist.

Not all transgenders embrace atheism, of course. Some claim to be living in accordance with God's will and preach a gospel of tolerance and acceptance of the LGBTQ ideology. But an increasing number embrace atheism because it is easier to justify the LGBTQ lifestyle if you are unaccountable to a higher authority.

As atheist Dallas Mitchell notes, "Authority—especially divine authority, corrupts and twists our innate moral goodness. At best, it divorces us from real moral accountability, turns morality into a mysterious object which can only be provided by a person's god."[32] If, as Mitchell asserts, moral goodness is innate, then the individual determines what is good and evil.

He explains, "What we [atheists] call 'immoral' or 'bad' or 'evil'—is that which causes harm. That which kills unnecessarily, that which injures, maims, causes pain and suffering. That which is detrimental to human well-being. That which leads to ignorance, stupidity, illiteracy, loss of freedom, enslavement, pain, unhappiness, poverty and anguish. That which leads to the opposite of all that is what we refer to as 'moral' or 'good.'"[33]

So even though atheists deny the existence of God, they believe evil is the opposite of good.

EVIL: PATH TO DESTRUCTION

If evil proves that God does not exist, then by the same reasoning, the existence of good must prove God does exist. When

---

[32] "Do Atheists Believe in Good and Evil? If so, on What Authority?" Quora, accessed March 14, 2024, https://www.quora.com/Do-atheists-believe-in-good-and-evil-If-so-on-what-authority.

[33] "Do Atheists Believe in Good and Evil?"

humans deny God's existence or begin to question His authority to define good and evil, they leave themselves open to accepting Satan's lies and the path of destruction he wishes them to follow. As Jesus said, "Wide is the gate and broad is the road that leads to destruction, and many enter through it" (Matthew 7:13).

In truth, Satan comes to kill and destroy the heart and soul of every human being, laughing all the while at those who choose their own way instead of God's ways (John 10:10). Indeed, what Mitchell identifies as evil—"that which is detrimental to human well-being"—is exactly what the Bible says about evil—it will lead to destruction.

The person looking to escape from biological gender generally is running from something—some event, relationship, or unmet need that has led to their brokenness and pain. They recognize the evil done to them, but they cannot see the source of that evil is connected to Satan's lies rather than God's truth.

WHY DOES GOD ALLOW EVIL?

For many in pain, this question arises: Why does God allow such pain and evil in the world? Let's explore a few reasons.

First of all, if God decided to do away with all the evil, we would lose free will. In the Garden of Eden, He provided Adam and Eve the opportunity to choose obedience or disobedience. They chose disobedience. "Therefore, just as sin entered the world through one man [Adam], and death through sin, and in this way death came to all people, because all sinned" (Romans 5:7). In one sense, evil exists in the world because human beings keep choosing to sin—to disobey what God has established as the standard of good.

Second, if God destroyed all evil, that would actually defeat the purpose for which you and I were created: "Everyone who is called by my name, whom I created for my glory, whom I formed and made" (Isaiah 43:7). We are created to bring glory to God. How do we do that? By choosing to love Him, choosing to obey Him. If the opportunity to choose evil didn't exist, we couldn't delight God and honor Him by making godly choices.

In the end, God will do away with all evil. He will cast Satan and his demons into the lake of fire so they can no longer tempt us to sin or wield sin as a weapon of destruction (Revelation 20:10). God will also bring all His people to the heavenly home He has prepared for them, where "there will be no more death or mourning or crying or pain, for the old order of things has passed away" (Revelation 21:4). In heaven, we will be forever free from the presence of sin and the desire to yield to it.

But for now, we have a daily choice to make—to love and obey God or to allow our fleshly emotions and sin nature to create a distance, and sometimes an eternity, away from Him.

TAKING RESPONSIBILITY

When people deny God's existence, they generally have had some terrible experience that leads them to think if there is a God, He is cruel to allow this or that to happen. Others have sown seeds of resentment and anger toward God for the pain and hardship they have allowed to enter their life.

Pain is inescapable. We cannot take a vacation and expect the wounds of the heart to disappear. The effects of these wounds are profound. No one can deny their desire for pain to simply disappear, and we look for escape from it in many ways.

Some use their pain as an excuse to remove God from their reality. It fuels the flame of doubt and sometimes undermines a Christian's faith. Sadly, this is what happens to many families enduring a long journey with a loved one identifying as transgender or homosexual. Their hearts swell up from the pain. The person who is lost in Satan's delusions about their identity also tries many coping mechanisms that lead them further away from reality and from God.

We may blame God for our evil actions that, quite honestly, we freely chose to pursue. We may also choose to avoid Him because of the fleshly desires that have taken over our life. We may excuse the actions as harmless, or we may accuse God when we suffer the natural consequences of those actions.

Taking responsibility for our choices is the first step toward changing our view of God. He is not the source of evil or of our pain. When we take that step, He is able to redirect us so we can begin to think of the impossible as possible: we are not slaves to our sinful desires; we are free to obey God instead.

The free will to choose to love God more than we love ourselves is one of God's greatest gifts to us. Through the redemption provided by Jesus, we can have victory over evil:

> So I find this law at work: Although I want to do good, evil is right there with me. For in my inner being I delight in God's law; but I see another law at work in me, waging war against the law of my mind and making me a prisoner of the law of sin at work within me. What a wretched man I am! Who will rescue me from this body that is subject to [sin and] death?

> Thanks be to God, who delivers me through Jesus Christ our Lord! (Romans 7:21–24)

THE SIN OF DENIAL

Denying the existence of evil allows us to excuse any action. Everything becomes permissible if I erase the idea that some behaviors are beneficial and some are detrimental.

Denial of evil not only blinds us to the truth, but it also leads us down a dangerous path of serving self rather than the Creator. Denial is not just a verbal response. It also manifests in actions and attitudes. In denying Christ, we deny His sacrifice, love, and grace. Yet, the reverse is equally strong—acknowledging Christ brings eternal affirmation.

Some Christians think they would never deny Jesus as Peter did. But we can be just as guilty as Peter if we allow a swelled-up heart full of pain and resentment to control us. Peter's denial was motivated by fear. We can yield to the sin of denial by making ungodly decisions or by permitting fleshly desires to run our life instead of yielding to God's plan for our life.

As we reflect on the time leading up to Peter's denial, we are reminded of the Last Supper, when Jesus Christ and His disciples had just finished their meal. At that time, Jesus revealed Judas Iscariot as the apostle who would betray Him. As if that wasn't difficult enough for His followers to process, Jesus then predicted that they would all abandon him. Their hearts must have pounded heavily as they could not imagine denying the One they loved and served.

Peter vowed that he would always be loyal to Jesus. He said, "Lord, I am ready to go with you to prison and to death"

(Luke 22:33). Peter had studied with Jesus, knew Jesus's heart and His ways. He loved Jesus so very much, so he likely could not fathom that he would deny Jesus once, let alone three times.

Later that same night, when the mob arrived to arrest Jesus in the Garden of Gethsemane—right where Judas told them He would be—Peter drew his sword and cut off the ear of Malchus, the high priest's servant, to show his allegiance to Jesus. But Jesus told Peter to put his sword away (Luke 22:50–51).

After Jesus had been arrested and taken away, Peter followed the mob to the courtyard of Caiaphas. Then the unthinkable happened to Peter. A servant girl saw him warming himself by a fire and accused Peter of being with Jesus. Peter immediately denied it. Later, he was again accused of being with Jesus and denied it again. Finally, a third person said Peter's Galilean accent gave him away as a follower of the Nazarene. Calling curses down on himself, Peter vehemently denied he knew Jesus. At that moment a rooster crowed. When he heard it, Peter went out and wept bitterly (Luke 22:54–62).

Can you imagine Peter living three years as a disciple of Jesus, then living through what likely was his most heartbreaking and unimaginable act—denying Jesus three times?

We may say, "I'd never do that," but the truth is we are capable of anything, even the things we do not want to do (Romans 7:15–19).

THE GREATEST GOOD

After Jesus's resurrection, Peter and six other disciples were fishing on the Sea of Galilee (John 21:1–3). Peter was surrounded by water and fishing, just like the first time he met Jesus and became one of His "fishers of men" (Matthew 4:19 NKJV).

When Peter saw Jesus, he jumped into the water and swam to shore to meet Him (John 21:7). Peter had done the unthinkable in denying his Lord, but out of his hunger to be with Jesus, to see him, Peter dove into the water to get to Jesus on the shore.

After they shared a meal, Jesus said to Simon Peter, "Simon son of John, do you truly love me more than these?" Peter responded, "Yes, Lord, you know that I love you." Jesus said, "Feed my lambs." Again Jesus said, "Simon son of John, do you truly love me?" He answered, "Yes, Lord, you know that I love you" (John 21:15–16).

Peter's story demonstrates that despite our weaknesses, failures, and sins, Jesus Christ waits for us to come seek Him for forgiveness and restore our relationship with Him. Some, like Peter, deny their relationship with Jesus, and some, like Dallas Mitchell, deny His existence and authority over their lives. Jesus's heart aches for them all, and He desires to restore them all, not tear them down like Satan does. As 2 Peter 3:9 says, "The Lord is not slow in keeping his promise, as some understand slowness. Instead he is patient with you, not wanting anyone to perish, but everyone to come to repentance."

Throughout history, those that considered themselves atheists and those who have said, "I no longer believe in God," have come back to Him. The flesh may have won out for a long time, but the person who comes back to their Creator is given more than he or she ever imagined possible—hope, peace, goodness, and love.

Good and Evil

In *The Problem of Pain*, C. S. Lewis observes, "God is the only good of all creatures . . . that there could be any other good, is an atheistic dream."[34] Don't buy into Satan's lie that you have the authority to determine what is good or evil apart from God. Don't allow Satan to delude you into thinking that good exists apart from God or that evil doesn't exist.

The greatest evil of all is refusing the greatest good ever offered—the salvation Jesus Christ provides and the freedom He alone can give.

If you're struggling with definitions of good and evil, talk to your loving heavenly Father about it. Open your heart to receive what He says. Study what the Bible says about good and evil, then use the verses you find as the measuring stick against what our culture says. Jesus died and rose again "to redeem us from all wickedness and to purify himself a people that are his very own, eager to do what is good" (Titus 2:14).

Are you eager to do what is good? Let Him lead you forward to that goal.

---

[34] C. S. Lewis, *The Problem of Pain* (New York: McMillan, 1962) 53.

CHAPTER SEVEN

A CRITICAL SPIRIT

Criticism. You may immediately have a negative reaction to that word. Most of us do. Even *Merriam-Webster* lists "the act of criticizing usually unfavorably" as the word's primary definition.[35] Few, if any of us, enjoy hearing unfavorable comments about our actions, appearance, beliefs, dreams, or desires. The comments may be true, but that doesn't make them more welcome. And if they're false, they can cause long-term damage.

Words are almost never neutral. They either inspire us or injure us. They either build up or tear down. The Bible says a lot about the way we speak to and about others. Two verses from the book of Proverbs highlight the damage and the healing words can bring about:

> The words of the wicked lie in wait for blood, but the speech of the upright rescues them. (Proverbs 12:6)

> The words of the reckless pierce like swords, but the tongue of the wise brings healing. (Proverbs 12:18)

The word *critical* can mean "inclined to criticize severely and unfavorably," but it can also mean "exercising or involving

---

[35] "Criticism," Merriam-Webster Online Dictionary, accessed May 15, 2024, https://unabridged.merriam-webster.com/collegiate/criticism.

careful judgment or judicious evaluation."[36] Satan wants us to use our words to injure and sometimes destroy another person. God wants us to use our words to inspire others and help them grow into the people He designed them to be.

SATAN'S SINISTER SPEECH SNARE

You're probably familiar with the term *critical spirit*. GotQuestions.org defines it as "prone to complaining, seeing the glass as half-empty, ruing unmet expectations, sensing failure (in others more than in oneself), and being judgmental."[37] A critical spirit is often manifested in the expression of disapproval of someone or something based on perceived faults or mistakes. In many cases, someone acts out of a critical spirit to harm another by passing judgment on a fault or placing blame. Those who give free rein to a critical spirit tear down other people rather than build them up. Over time, a person who is the target of this unwarranted disapproval may feel unworthy, unloved, or unaccepted. Satan uses someone's critical spirit as a snare to destroy both the inflictor and the recipient.

The Bible repeatedly warns against a critical spirit. Romans 14:10–13 instructs us wisely: "You, then, why do you judge your brother or sister? Or why do you treat them with contempt? For we will all stand before God's judgment seat. . . . Therefore let us stop passing judgment on one another. Instead, make up your mind not to put any stumbling block or obstacle in the way of a brother or sister." This passage highlights one of

---

[36] "Critical," Merriam-Webster Online Dictionary, accessed May 15, 2024, https://unabridged.merriam-webster.com/collegiate/critical.

[37] "How Can I Overcome Having a Critical Spirit?" GotQuestions.org, accessed May 15, 2024, https://www.gotquestions.org/critical-spirit.html.

the adverse effects of unjust criticism: it can construct a stumbling block, which prevents someone from receiving salvation or growing in their faith. Sadly, I've witnessed the devastating results a critical spirit can have on an innocent person who has not measured up in some way to other people's expectations.

Have you ever noticed we tend to judge people who may not appear to look or act man or woman enough? In conversations with hurting and broken people, I often hear how someone's critical spirit—often that of a loved one or other authority figure—has wreaked havoc in a vulnerable person's life. For example, a young boy appears more feminine in his mannerisms, perhaps the way he moves his hand through his hair with his fingers flickering. His speech is noticeably different—his voice too high or too soft. The critical spirit of others comes at him as if they are fighting a fierce war. They hurl accusations at him such as "You're gay" or "You're such a girl" or "You're a fag" or "Go kill yourself."

These destructive words crush the young boy's spirit. He begins to believe the critical, damaging words spoken to him and over him. He isn't strong enough to combat the emotional turmoil he's experiencing. The wounds inflicted by other people's critical spirits remain deep in his heart. The old saying "sticks and stones may break my bones, but words will never hurt me" is probably one of Satan's most dangerous lies as well as one of his most effective speech snares. Words don't damage the body; they damage the mind and the soul. And these emotional and mental wounds may take years to heal.

So the destructive words take root in the young boy's mind and heart. Before long, he doesn't just believe he is different from his male peers. He believes that he should not be male. God must have made a mistake, so he begins to live a life based on lies spoken over him. As the years pass, the young boy becomes a young man who not only believes he is different, but also seeks ways to get rid of the pain and become a new creation. After all, if the boys (or men) won't accept or bring him into their fold, his new creation will allow him to be part of the group where he's most comfortable and accepted—among girls. Girls are usually nurturers. They sympathize with the young boy and create a safer environment than combative males do.

A critical spirit can also have damaging effects on a girl. Like the young boy, she is rejected by others with a critical spirit. Maybe her facial features are not as feminine or as delicate as those of other girls. Perhaps her body is not as well developed in some areas like those of other girls her age. Her body type might not align with what society deems desirable in a woman. She doesn't look like the cheerleaders or homecoming queens in her school. Whispers begin: "Look at her, she's chubby" or "She doesn't wear makeup" or "She looks more like a boy than a girl."

These words inject poison into the mind and soul of the young girl searching to be accepted and embraced as she is—female. The unjust judgment of others makes her doubt that she's a girl. Why isn't she pretty like the popular girls? Why isn't she good enough to be included in their group?

And so the poisonous weeds of self-doubt and self-hatred take root in this girl's heart. Feeling ostracized by other girls, she also begins to live a life based on the lies spoken over her. She spirals downward into gender dysphoria and pursues hormone treatments, hoping that adopting a male persona will stop the pain raging within her.

FREEDOM FROM THIS SNARE

For the person who is damaged by other people's critical spirits, the healing begins with an understanding of their God-given identity. As I mentioned in chapter one, each person is divinely designed by God with a unique set of talents and abilities. No other person—past, present, or future—is the same as any other person. When God fashions a human being in a woman's womb, he creates that individual with a specific purpose and gives him or her a specific role in the kingdom of God.

For example, God told the prophet Jeremiah, "Before I formed you in the womb I knew you, before you were born I set you apart" (1:5). God appointed Jeremiah as "a prophet to the nations" (1:5). Likewise, God has given every person one or more spiritual gifts that are to be used for God's glory and to bring about His will on earth (see 1 Corinthians 12:4–11). Ephesians 4:11–13 explains the purpose of these gifts: to build up the body of Christ "until we all reach unity in the faith and in the knowledge of the Son of God and become mature, attaining to the whole measure of the fullness of Christ."

The next step in healing a mind and soul damaged by others' unjust criticism is embracing God's unconditional love. Our Creator loves each person because He created each person. And as Paul states in Romans 8:38–39, no one and nothing can separate us from that love:

> For I am convinced that neither death nor life, neither angels nor demons, neither the present nor the future,

> nor any powers, neither height nor depth, nor anything else in all creation, will be able to separate us from the love of God that is in Christ Jesus our Lord.

Hurting people living under the darkness of someone else's critical spirit need to know their value to God, and they need to receive praises for the unique talents and abilities they possess. The critical spirit of other people has done much harm and stolen much from far too many for far too long. God's heart and intention is for those wounded by others' judgmental words to experience His deep love and feel the pure, unconditional love that flows from His heart for them.

THE SELF-DESTRUCTIVE NATURE OF A CRITICAL SPIRIT

People who have a critical spirit don't just hurt others. They hurt themselves too. Their judgmental words often flow from their own need to feel empowered or to feel superior to others. By picking someone else apart and making that person feel and believe he or she has less value, the one with a critical spirit experiences a temporary false superiority. Someone operating out of this spirit is not aligning themselves with God and His heart.

The first-century Christians in Corinth liked to play the comparison game. Paul told them, "When they measure themselves by themselves and compare themselves with themselves, they are not wise" (2 Corinthians 10:12). Trying to build ourselves up by putting others down is unwise because it makes us the measuring stick of approved behavior, opinions, and skills. And we are not the measuring stick. Jesus Christ is, and our only goal should be to allow the Holy Spirit to make us more like Jesus.

The person suffering from a critical spirit is allowing Satan to deceive them into thinking more highly of themselves than they ought (Romans 12:3). Thankfully, God's ability to build us up is much more powerful than Satan's schemes to tear down God's creation in an attempt to destroy each person he can. Satan loves to trip people up, and he will go to great lengths to do so.

HELP FOR PERSON WITH A CRITICAL SPIRIT

The remedy for a critical spirit is the Holy Spirit.

First, admit that your critical spirit is a sin. Confess it and claim God's promise: "If we confess our sin, he is faithful and just to forgive us our sin and to cleanse us from all unrighteousness" (1 John 1:9).

Second, ask the Holy Spirit to search your heart and uproot any prideful attitudes that make you feel superior to others and ask Him to replace that pride with a clearer understanding of who you are in Christ—redeemed and beloved, set apart to serve Him and serve others in gratitude for all He has done for you.

Invite the Holy Spirit to cultivate His fruit in you—love, joy, peace, patience, goodness, kindness, faithfulness, gentleness, and self-control (Galatians 5:22–23). You may even want to put up a list of His fruit where you'll see it often.

In Psalm 141:3, David wrote, "Set a guard over my mouth, Lord; keep watch over the door of my lips." That's a good prescription for overcoming a critical spirit. Ask the Holy Spirit to make you aware each time your speech veers toward destructive mode. Before you speak to those who are most likely to be the targets of your hurtful words, think of several encouraging things you could say instead. You may even want to make a list of positive remarks and review it regularly.

Memorize Proverbs 16:24 or at least post it in a prominent place like a bathroom mirror or the refrigerator door: "Gracious words are a honeycomb, sweet to the soul and healing to the bones." Ask the Holy Spirit to let His grace and healing flow through you to others.

FOLLOW JESUS'S EXAMPLE

Jesus is the quintessential model of criticism that heals. Yes, He spoke harshly to the self-righteous and the self-absorbed, but His goal was to help them see their sin and repent of it so they could become the people they were designed to be. To those who were wounded and broken, however, He spoke gently and compassionately to achieve the same goal: be who God designed you to be.

Consider the story of the woman accused of adultery in John 8. Her accusers considered themselves superior to her—they didn't commit the sin she did. Jesus forced them to confront their own sin by saying, "Let any one of you who is without sin be the first to throw a stone at her" (v. 7). To the broken and wounded woman he said, "Neither do I condemn you . . . Go now and leave your life of sin" (v. 11). Notice that He didn't say "Don't worry about your sin—it's okay" or "What you're doing isn't wrong." He acknowledged that her behavior was sinful and encouraged her to leave that lifestyle behind.

AVOID SATAN'S SNARE

Satan will tempt us to believe that we are the person someone with a critical spirit says we are. That is a lie. Satan will also try to blind us to the pride, hypocrisy, and self-righteousness that feed the critical spirit in our heart. Keep asking God to open your eyes to those sins.

Healing from the damage inflicted by a critical spirit and overcoming that destructive spirit in ourselves are possible only through allowing God to do His work in us. Thankfully, He is willing and able to do that tough work. Be encouraged with these promises:

> He is able to do immeasurably more than all we ask or imagine. (Ephesians 3:20)
>
> [He] is able to keep you from stumbling and to present you before his glorious presence without fault and with great joy. (Jude 1:24)

Embrace those promises, then share them with someone who needs to be encouraged.

CHAPTER EIGHT

LIFE OUT OF TRAUMA

Trauma is "an injury or wound to a living body caused by the application of external force or violence."[38] According to The American Association for the Surgery of Trauma, physical "trauma is the leading cause of death for individuals up to the age of 45 years," and there are almost "40,000 homicide and suicide deaths each year in the US."[39]

Those statistics are sobering, but the breadth and depth of psychological trauma cannot be fully documented because not all people who suffer from this kind of trauma seek professional help. According to Psychology Today, psychological trauma "is a person's experience of emotional distress resulting from an event that overwhelms the capacity to emotionally digest it. The precipitating event may be a one-time occurrence or a series of occurrences perceived as seriously harmful or life-threatening to oneself or loved ones."[40]

Those suffering from the effects of psychological trauma have difficulty reestablishing a healthy mindset and lifestyle. Medical professionals can help, but this kind of trauma has a spiritual

---

[38] "Trauma," Merriam-Webster Online Unabridged Dictionary, accessed May 15, 2024, https://unabridged.merriam-webster.com/unabridged/trauma.

[39] "Trauma Facts," The American Association for the Surgery of Trauma, accessed May 15, 2024, https://www.aast.org/resources/trauma-facts.

[40] "What Is Trauma?" Psychology Today, accessed May 15, 2024, https://www.psychologytoday.com/us/basics/trauma#:~:text=Psychological%20trauma%20is%20a%20person's,to%20oneself%20or%20loved%20ones.

dimension that requires God's intervention. Because of this, it is essential to directly address a person's faith life whether the trauma was caused by abuse (mental, physical, or emotional) or by circumstances such as a parent dying when the person was young, or being bullied, or navigating a painful divorce.

SATAN'S ABUSIVE USE OF TRAUMA

As I've mentioned several times, Satan's goal is to destroy any and every aspect of God's creation. He targets human beings because we are made in the image of God, and anything Satan can do to mar that image in us, he will attempt—including trauma. He has no scruples. As far as he is concerned, the more injured we are, the better. And the longer he can keep us in that wounded, desperate state the easier it is for him to prevent us from becoming the people God designed us to be.

None of us should feel guilt or shame because we suffer from physical or psychological trauma. But we must be aware that Satan wants to use trauma to his advantage. He will tell us lies to keep us chained to the trauma, he will deceive us into thinking we cannot move past the trauma, and he will prompt us to use trauma as an excuse to indulge in sinful behaviors.

One lie Satan often tells us is that we must attach the blame for trauma to someone. It may seem easier to think that things always happen for a reason than to accept that accidents happen, and that bad things can be just that—bad. And maybe, it is also easier to think that if we struggle with life, if bad things happen to us, it is somehow our fault, because then there is the possibility that we could do something to change or avoid it. This kind of narrative quickly makes those who do not fit the patterns of so-called normal life conclude that they no longer belong, and this assumption adds to the trauma and distress of their experience.

Accepting that a lot of life is simply beyond our control can make our faith walk difficult during times of struggle. If we cling to a narrative that largely demands we deserve and receive blessings for our faith and faithfulness, what shallow faith we have.

On the night before Jesus's crucifixion, He told the Twelve, "I have told you these things, so that in me you may have peace. In this world, you will have trouble. But take heart! I have overcome the world" (John 16:33). We will have trouble. But Jesus has overcome the world so we can access His peace. Claim that promise daily.

TRAUMA IN THE BIBLE

Many characters in the Bible faced trauma. When a woman has experienced sexual abuse, we are reminded of the brutal sexual violence inflicted on women such as Dinah (Genesis 34) and Tamar (2 Samuel 13). Other examples of trauma are the parental horror of infants and toddlers being killed by power hungry, paranoid rulers such as Pharaoh in Exodus 1–2 and Herod in Matthew 2. Joseph's brothers sold him into slavery (Genesis 37), and King Saul hunted David like an animal for years (1 Samuel 19–24, 26–30).

David and other psalmists continually cry out to God in their distress, begging Him to rescue them. In Psalm 22:2 David says, "My God, I cry out by day, but you do not answer, by night, but I find no rest." And in Psalm 84:2 another writer says, "My souls yearns, even faints, for the courts of the LORD; my heart and my flesh cry out for the living God!"

Of course Jesus is the ultimate example of an innocent person traumatized by others. On the cross, he cried out, "My God, my God, why have you forsaken me?" (Matthew 27:46). No trauma we could ever experience compares with Jesus bearing the weight of every person's sins. And so we can confidently take our trauma to Him, knowing that He understands the depth of our pain and is able to navigate us through it to a place of hope and healing.

JOB'S JOURNEY THROUGH AND BEYOND TRAUMA

Although many Christians avoid Job's story due to the inexplicable hardship he endured, studying the way Job navigated trauma can help us navigate ours. Reverend Isabelle Hamley explores Job's journey through and beyond trauma in an insightful article written for Sanctuary Health Ministries, which connects Job's journey to ours.

Job's faith in God was founded on this principle: God blesses those who obey Him and punishes those who don't. Then Job lost his children and wealth and health (Job 1:13–19; 2:7). Initially, Job responds to his traumatic experience by saying, "The Lord has given, the Lord has taken away, blessed be the name of the Lord (Job 1:21). But, as Hamley notes, "Job is not engaging with the depth of his pain or trauma—yet. In terms of grief, he is in the denial stage. He cannot engage with what has happened."[41] This is Job's first response—as is true of many who experienced trauma.

---

[41] Rev. Isabelle Hamley, "Trauma and Belonging in the Book of Job," Sanctuary Mental Health Ministries, October 26, 2023, https://

She also observes that in the immediate aftermath of Job's trauma, he "reaches for words that are familiar, words that connect him to the faith he shares with others."[42] He does what we often do in a crisis—mouth platitudes. "God works all things together for good" or "God never makes mistakes." But I think we'd all agree that these platitudes aren't helpful. In fact, they often aggravate a suffering person's anger or confusion. The common thinking that Job's friends share doesn't help him either.

Trauma robs Job of his speech and the language and stories that help him connect with his family and peers.[43] When his friends arrive, the group is so overwhelmed by what has happened to Job, a godly man, that they sit silent for an entire week: "Then they sat on the ground with him for seven days and seven nights. No one said a word to him, because they saw how great his suffering was" (Job 2:13).

Although Job is a faithful servant of God, he cannot explain the unpredictable, intense suffering he endures. Like many of us do, he wrestles with the idea that a good God could allow such hardship. He cries out, "I have no peace, no quietness; I have no rest, but only turmoil" (Job 3:26).

"When Job's body starts to fail—a natural bodily response to the immense trauma he is facing—this moves Job to a different place. He asks, 'Shall we accept good from God, and not trouble?'"[44]

---

sanctuarymentalhealth.org/2023/10/26/trauma-and-belonging-in-the-book-of-job/.

[42] Hamley, "Trauma and Belonging in the Book of Job."

[43] Hamley, "Trauma and Belonging in the Book of Job."

[44] Hamley, "Trauma and Belonging in the Book of Job."

(Job 2:10). Doubts arise as he attempts to find a reason for his suffering and push him toward anger, then despair. "Why did I not perish at birth, and die as I came from the womb? . . . For now I would be lying down in peace; I would be asleep and at rest"(Job 3:11–13).

Hamley rightly notes, "The Word of God does not sugarcoat the effects of trauma; it does not gloss over the reality of despair. Job is as low as a person can get. He feels so alone and alienated that he wishes all connections with friends, family, and God to cease. He wishes for darkness alone . . . Suffering isolates, it cuts off bonds of fellowship and can make people feel that they are alone and simply do not belong. . . . Job rants and raves and complains and takes God to task"[45] in his desperation to make sense of the trauma he has experienced. "Job rebels against all that he used to believe about the world being ordered,"[46] like many who say they once had faith but no longer identify with that faith. Somehow, they find it more soothing to believe there is no God than to accept that the Almighty God works in ways that we cannot fully understand.

"Job is lost in a world that he no longer understands," Hamley observes. "He cannot see order or safety, and he complains bitterly to God and his friends that he is innocent and should never have suffered."[47] He says, "I cry out to you, O God, but you do not answer; I stand up, but you merely look at me. You turn on me ruthlessly; with the might of your hand you attack me" (Job 30:20–21).

---

[45] Hamley, "Trauma and Belonging in the Book of Job."

[46] Hamley, "Trauma and Belonging in the Book of Job."

[47] Hamley, "Trauma and Belonging in the Book of Job."

Not until God reminds Job of His power and sovereignty does Job accept that he must trust God even though he does not understand Him or His ways at all. When God has finished speaking, Job says,

> I know that you can do all things;
> No plan of yours can be thwarted.
> You asked, "Who is this that
> Obscures my counsel without knowledge:
> Surely, I spoke of things I did not understand,
> Things too wonderful for me to know. (Job 42:2–3)

And that is the mindset we must all embrace if we are to move beyond trauma. We must trust God's unconditional love for us when we don't understand His ways. We must focus on His unchanging attributes of goodness, wisdom, and faithfulness. But how do we get there?

THE HOPE OF HEALING

Though someone may believe their shattered heart is impossible to mend, it is not. God repairs the pieces of the broken heart through His loving and dedicated heart. Psalm 147:3 says, "He heals the brokenhearted and binds up their wounds."

Faith in Christ and a relationship with Him brings the healing and peace every traumatized person desires. For those who experienced abandonment, Christ is there for them and deeply desires for them to know Him more intimately so that He is invited into the false belief that no one was or is there for them.

God not only brings healing to the physical body but also to the mind and to the soul. As Exodus 15:26 says, He is our *Jehovah*

Rapha—the God who heals us and delivers us from any brokenness so we can become whole in Christ.

Psalm 34:18 says, "The Lord is close to the brokenhearted and saves those who are crushed in spirit." The word *brokenhearted* brings to mind an image of a shattered mirror, shards of glass scattered everywhere. This reminds us of how difficult it is to put a life back together after trauma.

The verses that follow assure the brokenhearted person that "the righteous person may have many troubles, but the Lord delivers him from them all" (v. 19). And the psalm ends with this promise: "The Lord will rescue his servants; no one who takes refuge in him will be condemned" (v. 22). God showers mercies on us daily as we process the reality of our situation and navigate the pain inflicted on our body, soul, and heart. Isaiah 53:5 also affirms the hope of healing: "But he was pierced for our transgressions; he was crushed for our iniquities; upon him was the chastisement that brought us peace, and with his wounds we are healed."

Though these scriptures are comforting, there is much work to be done by the Holy Spirit and God's people to help someone come out of the trauma, no matter what they experienced, and into the peace God has for them.

NAVIGATING YOUR TRAUMA

Allowing God into your trauma is essential, and answering two questions is a vital first step: Am I going to allow trauma and the scars to dictate the rest of my life through shame, guilt, and owning false truths about myself? Or am I willing to hand the trauma over to God and allow Him to deliver, rescue, and protect me?

I hear stories from people who feel crushed by the weight of what they carry without knowing how to get rid of it, especially when they have bought Satan's message of being born in the wrong body—a lie often fed to a hurting, shattered heart. It doesn't matter what we've faced, Jesus Christ can provide the physical, emotional, and psychological healing we need.

Jesus told His disciples that because of the sin and brokenness in this world, we will face trials (John 16:33). The curses and tragedies that we will most probably face are due to our sin and others' sins as well as Satan's deceptions and lies—such as the one he whispers into the hearts of those who believe God made a mistake in their biological sex.

One important step toward healing is remembering and clinging to this promise: God "will cover you with his feathers. He will shelter you with his wings. His faithful promises are your armor and protection" (Psalm 91:14 NLT). Holding on to this truth can be challenging when a person's conception of God's free will leads them to blaming God for allowing the trauma experienced.

The traumas many endure who identify as trans are often hidden deep in their heart and soul, prompting their desire to blame God for what was done and what was not stopped. But as the person comes to a deeper understanding of who God is and who He isn't, a clearer picture is brought into the light. Through His faithful love and support, even the worst trauma can lead to healing, if the person is willing to see their circumstances through God's eyes, not their own. The Holy Spirit ministers deeply so fear of the unspoken or hidden events no longer control the person: Psalm 91 continues with this assurance: "You will not fear the terror of night, nor the arrow that flies by day, nor the pestilence that stalks in the darkness, nor the plague that destroys at midday" (vv. 5–6).

Come into the presence of God recognizing and fully believing He does hear you when you speak to Him. And yes, He does answer you (sometimes, though, not the way you wish). Many trauma victims fear God is not with them. They question the "why" of what they experienced: Why did God allow this to happen to me? What did I do to deserve this horror? Fear often prevents a person from coming forward and truly seeking God. After all, God's answer may not be what they desire to hear or read through the Word of God. But God says, "Fear not, for I am with you; be not dismayed, for I am your God; I will strengthen you, I will help you, I will uphold you with my righteous right hand" (Isaiah 41:10). He also promises, "But whoever listens to me will dwell secure and will be at ease, without dread of disaster" (Proverbs 1:33 ESV).

GOD'S DESIRE FOR US

The only way complete restoration and healing occur is by making Jesus Christ the center of our life. Isaiah 61:2–4 tells us about the Lord's favor toward us and His desire to comfort us:

> To proclaim the acceptable year of the Lord,
> And the day of vengeance of our God;
> To comfort all who mourn,
> To console those who mourn in Zion,
> To give them beauty for ashes,

Life Out of Trauma

> The oil of joy for mourning,
> The garment of praise for the spirit of heaviness;
> That they may be called trees of righteousness,
> The planting of the LORD, that He may be glorified.
> And they shall rebuild the old ruins,
> They shall raise up the former desolations,
> And they shall repair the ruined cities,
> The desolations of many generations.

Instead of mourning your loss, instead of walking in a spirit of grieving and mourning, receive and experience God's comfort. Permit the Holy Spirit to gather those shattered pieces of your life caused by trauma, allow Him to turn your trauma into a garland of beauty instead of ashes for the entirety of your life.

Are you feeling as low as Job felt in the middle of his trauma? Are you crying out to God but feel like He has turned His back on you while you sit in a pile of ashes, scraping your skin with broken pieces of pottery?

God wants you to exchange the ashes for a garland of beauty. He offers a garment of praise instead of the heaviness you're living under. He can and will set you free from the trauma that's crushing your heart and spirit.

CHAPTER NINE

EXPOSING THE DARKNESS

When God created the world, one of the first things He did was dispel the darkness:

> Now the earth was formless and empty, darkness was over the surface of the deep, and the Spirit of God was hovering over the waters. And God said, "Let there be light," and there was light. God saw that the light was good, and he separated the light from the darkness. (Genesis 1:2–4)

Light and darkness cannot coexist. Light always drives away darkness. And in our fight against the darkness Satan loves, we must dedicate ourselves to living in the light. The key to living in the light is to develop our spiritual eyesight so we can distinguish between God's light and Satan's darkness. In Ephesians 1:18–19, Paul offers this prayer: "I pray that the eyes of your heart may be enlightened in order that you may know the hope to which he has called you, the riches of his glorious inheritance in his holy people, and his incomparably great power for us who believe."

Our physical eyes are God-designed to take in light. First, light passes through the cornea. Some of this light enters our pupil, and the iris controls how much light the pupil lets in. When light hits the retina, special cells turn the light into electrical signals that the brain turns into the images we see.[48] The eyes of our heart—our soul or innermost being—are designed to take in spiritual light. This light is manifested in God's Word (Psalm 119:105) and through Jesus, the Light of the World (John 8:12). The eyes of our heart tell us that spiritual light exists, and the Bible tells us that only God can move us out of spiritual darkness and into spiritual light:

> The god of this age [Satan] has blinded the minds of unbelievers, so that they cannot see the light of the gospel that displays the glory of Christ, who is the image of God. (2 Corinthians 4:4)

DARKNESS AND LIGHT

When someone lives in darkness, they experience the absence of light. We know what darkness is because we know what light is. Light, on the other hand, is not dependent on darkness to exist. The apostle John said, "The light shines in the darkness, and the darkness has not overcome it" (John 1:5). Something can obstruct the sun's light and produce a shadow that makes our surroundings dim, but the obstruction does not—cannot—extinguish the sun. Neither can the spiritual darkness generated by our sin and Satan's lies ever extinguish the light of God's truth.

Our very experience of spiritual darkness bears witness to the existence of spiritual light just as a shadow proves the sunshine. And if that's true, seeking the sun instead of the shadows is where we find satisfying spiritual life. Jesus said, "I am the light of the world. Whoever follows me will never walk in darkness,

---

[48] Adapted from "How the Eyes Work," National Eye Institute, accessed May 21, 2024, https://www.nei.nih.gov/learn-about-eye-health/healthy-vision/how-eyes-work.

but will have the light of life" (John 8:12). Jesus pairs light and life. Without light we cannot have life.

Of course, light not only reveals that which is hidden in darkness, but it also gives life and sustains it. We wouldn't be able to grow food without the light, and none of God's beauty could be seen and enjoyed without light. Think about a plant. It must have light to live. You cannot hide it in a dark closet and expect it to flourish. Every elementary school student learns about photosynthesis—the process by which plants use sunlight to synthesize nutrients from carbon dioxide and water.

When Jesus compares Himself to light and life, He's declaring that no fulfilling, productive life is possible without Him. But we can become so used to living in the shadows and darkness of our sinful behaviors that we avoid Jesus, the Light of the World, who gives us life.

ACCUSTOMED TO DARKNESS

When a person walks through the valley of shadows, how do they discern the shadows? If the person says, "Surely the darkness shall cover me, and the light about me be night" (Psalm 139:11), how can they still distinguish day from night?

Those shadows can be created by a number of events that took place in someone's life. The initial thought, reasoning, or action was the seed that sadly began to multiply with further lies and destruction in one's life, which led to more spiritual darkness.

Our spiritual eyesight can become so weak that we can't tell we're living in darkness. If you wake up in the middle of the night in a dark room, it takes a minute or two for your eyes to adjust to the darkness. Usually, though, they do adapt and images slowly emerge. If you remain in that darkened room long enough, you'll probably be able to function, but many objects will still remain undetected or unclear.

If people live in spiritual darkness long enough, they may think it is "freeing" them to be who they always were meant to be. The apostle Paul describes this state in Romans 1:20–21:

> For since the creation of the world God's invisible qualities—his eternal power and divine nature—have been clearly seen, being understood from what has been made [the natural realm], so that people are without excuse. For although they knew God, they neither glorified him nor gave thanks to him, but their thinking became futile and their foolish hearts were darkened.

The Amplified Bible says, "They became worthless in their thinking [godless, with pointless reasonings, and silly speculations], and their foolish heart was darkened" (v. 21).

The very suggestion of this freedom in darkness motivates people to deny the Creator His rightful place in their lives and to forfeit the true freedom of living in the light. They become susceptible to "silly speculations" such as these:

- God is okay with same-sex relationships, or He wouldn't have given me these feelings.
- If a person feels uncomfortable in his or her body, that person must be in the wrong body.
- Loving someone means that I must approve of all their decisions—even if those decisions are irrational and harmful.

The longer someone holds on to these dark delusions the more difficult it is for that person to distinguish light from darkness. And telling them their vision is 20/20 is hurting them, not helping them.

What is hidden in the darkness can only be revealed when light shines on it. By our willingness to walk in Christ, we allow the light of His holiness to penetrate the darkness that once took a person captive, living a life of slavery cunningly designed by the enemy, Satan. He attempts and sometimes claims victory in people due to their ignorance of the almighty and all-powerful God.

Even Satan's demons believe in God and in His Light. They also know the power of speaking His name: "You believe that there is one God. Good! Even the demons believe that—and shudder" (James 2:19).

CHOOSING TO LIVE IN THE LIGHT

In his first letter, the apostle John writes, "This is the message we have heard from him and declare to you: God is light; in him there is no darkness at all. If we claim to have fellowship with him yet walk in the darkness, we lie and do not live by the truth. But if we walk in the light, as he is in the light, we have fellowship with one another, and the blood of Jesus, his Son, purifies us from all sin" (1 John 1:5–7).

When John says that "God is light," he is literally saying God is the illuminator. He is the illuminator and creator of all that was, is, and ever will be. "In the beginning," when the earth was dark and void, God provided light for us (Genesis 1:1–3). His creation of physical light is symbolic of the spiritual illumination Jesus Christ brought when He walked on earth for thirty-three years and then gave His life so we could walk in the Light permanently. Through Jesus Christ, anyone living in darkness can see truth and reality through the Word of God. It is the Good News about the truth of God's love that is capable of overcoming any obstacle, no matter how dark.

John's use of the word *darkness* in 1 John 1:5 refers to all that is opposed to God. People oppose God and reject Him out of the darkness of their sin. But because His love is powerful enough to restore sight to the blind, we must never give up on God's uniqueness to bring healing into the shattered lives Satan has proclaimed victory over.

When we live with biblical hope, we have an anchored life. We are held steady in the midst of any storm or trauma experienced. Because hope is often misunderstood, an accurate understanding of the meaning of hope is crucial. The Bible says that when your hope is anchored in God, He will teach you His truth and lead you in the way you should go."[49]

The book of Psalms offers us instruction on how to achieve the results we desire when we feel hopeless. "Guide me in your truth and teach me, for you are God my Savior, and my hope is in you all day long" (Psalm 25:5). God guides us through His truths which leads to instruction, offering us the answer of where we find hope.

Let's be honest here. The world's brand of hope—wishful thinking and deceitful fantasies—merely masks unfilled and empty places within the heart. Deep inside we still crave to know the

---

[49] June Hunt, *Hope* (Torrance, CA: Aspire Press), 11.

One who does offer us real hope—confidence in His plan and His purpose for our lives.

Satan intends to use all that we have experienced through living hopelessly to steal all the plans God has for our healing. Satan wants us to believe that our pain has no purpose. But Romans 5:3–5 offers this piece of wisdom: "We also rejoice in our sufferings, because we know that suffering produces perseverance; perseverance, character; and character, hope. And hope does not disappoint us, because God has poured out his love into our hearts by the Holy Spirit, whom he has given us."

Do you want hope that lasts? The process is laid out clearly in these verses: allow God to develop perseverance and godly character in you. Asking God for His help is far better than any self-help you might have tried. Ask Him to increase your faith, or perhaps begin a new foundation of faith. Stop and listen to God. Believe the promises His Word offers you.

HELPING THOSE WHO LIVE IN DARKNESS

Often, we look at others through our physical eyes, yet so much could be gained by choosing to look at them through our spiritual lenses instead.

People trapped in an identity crisis are crying for help. Whether their cry is "I didn't see what was happening to me," or "Please help, I don't know a way out of this," their pain and confusion are real. They are trapped in darkness.

Unfortunately, many times we don't hear their cries or even recognize the reality of what they have been through. But God does! Helping the person to see God's great love and grace is essential to penetrating the darkness which imprisons them. In the dark, they try to rationalize why they do what they do, and they pretend God is really okay with transitioning. Pumping themselves full of drugs and undergoing radical surgeries appear to be the right choices—the only choices. All light has been shut out in their heart, and they yield to the dark deceptions that flow from their sinful heart, desires which will ultimately lead to their destruction.

The reminder that someone is walking in hopelessness breaks the heart of those standing on the sidelines. Helping others know the hope you may know and have experienced first means remembering God's faithfulness when you struggled yourself. Reach out with complete compassion, acknowledging where the person is and the hopelessness they are struggling with. God is merciful and patient with you. Extend that mercy and patience to others.

Sometimes we can know God's desires for us in our mind through Scripture or wise counsel. But embracing God's purposes and living them out still seems impossible. We can work very hard at doing what we, or other people, consider the right things. But Satan can use those good intentions to keep us in darkness. Why? When we focus on trying harder, we fail to realize it's not about *doing* but rather about *being* in a personal relationship with God. Trying harder will never work. Instead, we must release control to God. We must give Him first place in our life, forfeiting all other people and things that attempt to take His place as our Creator, Redeemer, and King.

Pray for the person who feels hopeless and tell them often that you are praying for them. Send a text or a handwritten note. Make a phone call. Trust God's plans for them and for you.

Deflect any arrows of unbelief Satan may hurl at you. He will say God's not listening and God doesn't care. He will tell you that God won't help the person you're praying for because that person's too far gone. Don't listen to him.

The world will offer nothing but hopelessness to the person believing Satan's lies, allowing him to imprison them in the darkness of sinful mindsets and behaviors. Only God's amazing love can bring darkened hearts into His light. Only He can open hearts to hear His voice and proclaim His truth over their lives. Only He can expose the darkness for what it is . . . nothing compared to the light Jesus offers.

CHAPTER TEN

LIVING IN THE LIGHT

Human beings walk the earth seeking completeness in their search to heal their own heart. Just ask Solomon, who had the wealth, wisdom, power, and opportunity to try every means possible to find fulfillment and still came to this conclusion: "Yet when I surveyed all that my hands had done and what I had toiled to achieve, everything was meaningless, a chasing after the wind; nothing was gained under the sun" (Ecclesiastes 2:11).

He tried everything. But gained nothing.

It's time to wake up.

We are not God. We are God's creation, and the only way to find completeness, to enjoy fulfillment is to be the person He designed us to be.

Time is an indefinite, continual progression of existence and events. The time of grace, forgiveness, and redemption is available to each human being. Sadly, some find it difficult to believe God loves them or that redemption and fulfillment in Christ Jesus is possible. This leads them down a path of unbelief and prevents their heart from truly healing.

They try everything. But gain nothing.

GET UP AND GET DRESSED

Romans 13 offers wisdom to the sleeping soul through Paul's warning: "Do this, understanding the present time: The hour has already come for you to wake up from your slumber, because our salvation is nearer now than when we first believed. The night is nearly over; the day is almost here" (vv. 11–12).

Paul reminds us that as Christians we are all "morning people." Right before dawn, the sky brightens, as if an alarm goes off to remind us that it's morning. Time to get up. The sunlight rouses us to begin the day and get out of bed. The time has also come to rouse our minds from spiritual slumber, to be alert to God's work in the world and to live in accordance with God's coming salvation.

When we wake up, we crawl out of bed and get dressed for the day. Paul tells us what to wear by instructing us to "put on the armor of light" and "put on the Lord Jesus Christ" (v. 12). I've often thought of our military folks doing all they can to protect the borders of our beloved country and the people living within it. Well-trained soldiers go through endless hours of training before entering the war zone. Once they've arrived at their camp, they wait for the right time to take their position to engage the enemy. They may sniff the wind or scan the horizon, fully clothed in their combat uniform with their weapons strapped on them.

This image conveys readiness for conflict, but for the purpose of understanding the importance of knowing our enemy and how to fight Satan, training is needed. In Ephesians 6:12, Paul clarifies that the enemy is not "flesh and blood" but "principalities . . . powers . . . the rulers of the darkness of this age . . . the spiritual hosts of wickedness in the heavenly places" (NKJV).

Some may scratch their heads and wonder how to make sense of this spiritual battle alongside their struggle with their identity and the freedom from bondage God desires them to walk in. But that confusion is caused by Satan's ability to blind people to what is truly going on—a spiritual war against God. The human quest for completeness and fulfillment is merely a means Satan uses to draw people into his army.

ENGAGE THE ENEMY

We must deliberately choose God's army instead. It is therefore time to "put aside the deeds of darkness and put on the armor of light" (Romans 13:12). We must walk in the light. How? Here's a start: "Let us behave decently, as in the daytime, not in carousing and drunkenness, not in sexual immorality and debauchery, not in dissension and jealousy" (Romans 13:13–14).

As Christians, we are to fight against the destructive powers that enslave and divide people. That might be a history of mistrust and injustice, addictions, thirst for revenge, prejudice, fear, greed, and so forth. Paul calls these "the works of the flesh" that result from "the desires of the flesh" (Galatians 5:17–19 ESV). Too often the petty manifestations of these powers erode our fellowship and our witness.

When we engage in battle against such destructive spirit-realm powers, we are fighting to take back what the enemy has or is attempting to steal from a person, such as their identity or the false belief that they are not loved or that they are too damaged to go to God. These heart issues prevent them from receiving the healing the Great Physician offers, and far too many continue to live under the bondage of a false identity, unable to live fully as God intended.

The only strategy that leads to victory in this spiritual war is to "clothe yourselves with the Lord Jesus Christ, and do not think about how to gratify the desires of the flesh" (Romans 13:14).

God desires that every single person He created wakes up and recognizes the time is now to accept Jesus Christ as their personal Lord and Savior and to discover the joy and healing of being bound up with their hope in Christ (see Luke 2:32; Romans 15:13). It is time to recognize that He has delivered them from their past sins and is willing to save them in the present from the power of sin over their lives. And lastly, He will save us in the **future** from the very presence of sin.

Satan wants to prevent you from living in the light of God's love, truth, and purpose. Follow the apostle Peter's advice instead.

> Be alert and of sober mind. Your enemy the devil prowls around like a roaring lion looking for someone to devour. Resist him, standing firm in the faith, because you know that the family of believers throughout the world is undergoing the same kind of sufferings. And the God of all grace, who called you to his eternal glory in Christ, after you have suffered a little while, will himself restore you and make you strong, firm and steadfast. To him be the power for ever and ever. Amen. (1 Peter 5:8–11)

Be alert. Resist the enemy. One of the most sobering facts about life is that all humans have a supernatural enemy whose aim is to use pain and pleasure to make us blind, stupid, and miserable—forever. The Bible calls him "the devil and Satan, the deceiver of the whole world ... the accuser" (Revelation 12:9–10), "the ruler of this world" (John 12:3), and "the god of this age" (2 Corinthians 4:4).

Preparation is key when it comes to resisting the enemy. Having a battle plan before the enemy strikes is instrumental in helping us combat the attacks and false beliefs he uses. He has his own battle plan for destroying a person, which makes it essential to know how to resist his destructive intentions.

If you begin to design your personal war plan by using the instruments God gives you through Scripture, you will be ready to implement your plan and win the battles that come your way. It isn't easy to identify when or where you are most vulnerable to the temptations and attacks, so utilize spiritual practices regularly. Prayer, meditation, and worship can establish a rhythm of spiritual discipline which builds your resilience over time. If you have no plan, the enemy laughs and likely wonders what kind of soldier goes into a war without a plan. The Lord Jesus Christ will give you the strength to fight and the wisdom to conquer any of the enemy's plans to take you down and out.

Stand firm. Know with full confidence that you can rely on the words and promises of God. The enemy loves to whisper lies to the person rejecting their gender. "You aren't good enough," "Transitioning will make you happy," or "You have the right to do with your body as you want." James says, "Resist the devil, and he will flee from you!" (James 4:7). But how do you manage that task?

According to Revelation 12:11, "They have conquered him by the blood of the Lamb and by the word of their testimony, for they loved not their lives even unto death" (ESV). These first-century Christians embraced the triumph of Christ, which He achieved by His blood on the cross. These Christians spoke that truth in faith. They did not fear death. They triumphed, and we can too as we allow the Holy Spirit to develop in us the same type of faith. Our testimony of what God does for us and in us is where we see our own transformation and healing by the power of the Holy Spirit. Rejoice in the Lord always and let your spirit of hope be known by the word of your testimony.

As you spend time with God in prayer and in His Word, He transforms you from the inside out—that is, if you have fully surrendered to Him. You can say you've fully surrendered to God, but in reality surrendering means letting go of the plans you have in your heart to seek a rebellious life through your Plan A or B. Don't give the enemy that foothold. Be anxious about nothing; instead be in prayer and be thankful (Philippians 4:6).

Satan's lies will fail. Far too often we fall for what Satan's message suggests. We understand the power he has over others when using their weak links, like Eve who thought she deserved to know all that God knows.

"When he lies, he speaks out of his own character, for he is a liar and the father of lies" (John 8:44 ESV). The first time Satan appears in the Bible in Genesis 3, his first words cast suspicion on the truth: "Did God actually say, 'You shall not eat of any tree in the garden'?" (Genesis 3:1). Do you see how the enemy twists things to make sense to you? A twisted thought might be "Surely, you deserve to do as you please," using an entitlement behavior.

The second words on his lips were a subtle falsehood: "You will not surely die" (Genesis 3:4 ESV). John says that Satan "does not stand in the truth, because there is no truth in him" (John 8:44 ESV). We are dealing with the essence of falsehood and deception. This is a never-ending trap leading nowhere but the path of destruction and taking away the plans God has for each person. Satan fears you, your worth, and the plans God has for you so much that he wants to destroy you. It is up to you! Will you allow him to destroy you, or will you choose to focus on how valuable you are to God and fight the enemy's lies with the truth of God?

If you stand with full confidence that you were fearfully and wonderfully made by a God who has plans for you to prosper, the enemy will have a tougher time knocking you down. Wholeness and peace come from God's Word and how He defines you.

God's truth will win. In The Living Bible, 2 Timothy 2:19–21 reads, "But God's truth stands firm like a great rock, and nothing can shake it. It is a foundation stone with these words written on it: 'The Lord knows those who are really his,' and 'A person who calls himself a Christian should not be doing things that are wrong.' In a wealthy home there are dishes made of gold and silver as well as some made from wood and clay. The expensive dishes are used for guests, and the cheap ones are used in the kitchen or to put garbage in. If you stay away from sin, you will be like one of these dishes made of purest gold—the very best in the house—so that Christ himself can use you for his highest purposes."

Jesus calls us to wartime prayer: "But stay awake at all times, *praying* that you may have strength to escape all these things that are going to take place, and to stand before the Son of Man" (Luke 21:36 ESV, emphasis added). Similarly, Peter makes an urgent call to end-time prayer: "The end of all things is at hand; therefore be self-controlled and sober-minded for the sake of *your prayers*" (1 Peter 4:7 ESV, emphasis added).

Even Jesus fought against the devil on our behalf with the weapon of prayer. He said to Peter in Luke 22:31–32, "Satan demanded to have you that he might sift you like wheat, but *I have prayed for you* that your faith may not fail" (ESV, emphasis added). So Jesus illustrates for us the opposition of a specific satanic threat with prayer.

Jesus instructed us to make prayer a daily weapon for protection in general: "Lead us not into temptation, but deliver us from the evil one" (Matthew 6:13). Jesus will deliver you from the successful temptation of the evil one. Go forth and use the power available to you. Develop a godly perspective and mindset. When the enemy attacks say, "Who do you think you are, messing with one of God's children?"

Walk in that power!

Other Books by Denise Shick

Non-Fiction

Moving Forward in Hope: A Devotional for Families of LGBTQ+ Loved Ones

When Hope Seems Lost: How to Deal with Transgenderism in the Church

Understanding Gender Confusion

Transgender Confusion – A Biblically Based Q&A for Families

Your True Identity: How Freedom in Christ Brings Healing, Hope, and Wholeness

My Daddy's Secret

Children's Books

When Daddy Leaves to Be a Girl

I Am Glad God Made Me a Girl

What's Up with Cousin Stacy?

The Boy Who Liked Tea Parties

Other Authors

Dangerous Affirmations: My Transgender Experience by Jerry Lake

Moving Forward in Hope is a collection of 90 devotions that can help you advance toward confidence in God's plan for you and your LGBTQ+ loved one. Today you may not know what to say to God, your loved one, or other people about this journey. You may feel angry, ashamed, bewildered, and adrift. Denise Shick has been there, and the people whose stories are shared in this devotional have been there. Their courage to step toward God, faith, and hope can inspire you to move forward too.

Denise Shick is thrilled to announce the release of *Moving Forward in Community*. The goal of this biblical tool is to come alongside you in your journey with a LGBTQ+ loved one. In this thirteen-week study, Denise and others share parts of their stories to meet you right where you are today and lift you up.

Your True Identity: How Freedom in Christ Brings Healing, Hope, and Wholeness provides a biblical perspective on gender and sexuality for those who struggle with gender identity, transsexual confusion, and same-sex or opposite-sex compulsions.

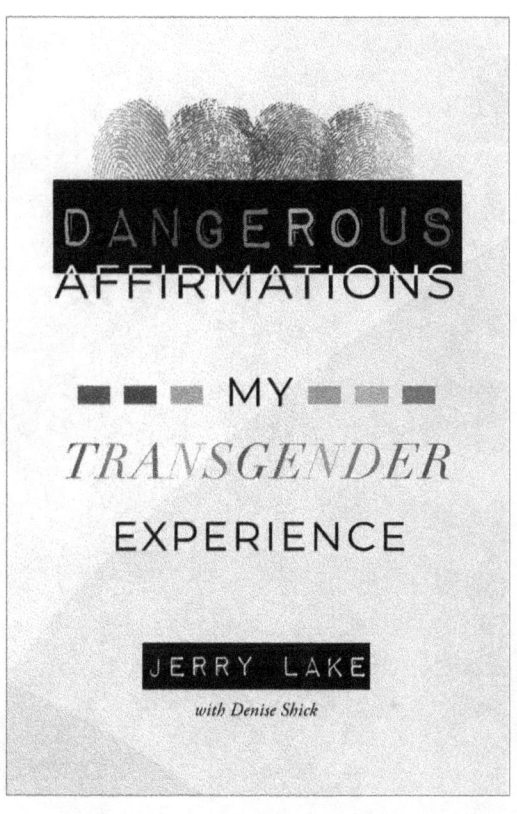

Dangerous Affirmations is a personal story of a young boy who shares his struggle of living in his male gender. As a child, his grandmother dressed him in a dress, while his father affirmed him looking pretty. ***Dangerous Affirmations*** addresses this from a Christian standpoint.

There is a great deal of mystery and confusion about how to deal with transgenderism in the Christian community. *When Hope Seems Lost* provides churches and families with a biblical response to transgenderism.

*Transgender Confusion –
A Biblically Based Q&A for Families*

Having a loved one who identifies as the opposite gender is challenging. Family members face situations that will stretch their emotional and spiritual strength. The Bible does not use the word transgenderism, but it does talk about our minds becoming a battlefield. So where do we go to bring clarity? We go to God's Word. He addresses the fleshly desires and reminds us "our struggle is not against flesh and blood, but against the rulers, against the authorities, against the powers of this dark world and against the spiritual forces of evil in the heavenly realms" (Ephesians 6:12–13).

Understanding Gender Confusion

Sometimes people think if they pray or wish hard enough, their transgender tendencies will disappear. This is an unrealistic expectation. It is not reasonable to expect an overnight change in the area of gender or sexual confusion. The problem takes years to develop. Likewise, the restoration process requires a lengthy healing and hard work, which typically involves years of serious commitment.

My Daddy's Secret is the sensitive, often heartbreaking, true story of the effects of a father's secret sexual addictions on his family—particularly on his oldest daughter, whom he made his confidante when she was just nine years old. The author hopes this book will provide new insights into the pain such addictions inflict on families and insight into God's amazing grace in healing those pains.

When Daddy Leaves to Be a Girl can help children handle the emotional turmoil of learning that their parent wants to transition to another sex. In age-appropriate language, Denise Shick explores the fears, confusion, and anger a child may experience during these difficult circumstances. She offers children assurance that God sees their pain and loves them. She also gives practical ways to guide children toward emotional and spiritual wholeness.

What's Up with Cousin Stacy? explores one family's response to the news of a loved one identifying as LGBTQ. With his parents' help, Kevin learns that love, honesty, and prayer are the best ways to navigate stressful situations.

This book is a valuable tool for parents, pastors, and counselors who seek to demonstrate love and compassion as they help families process and respond to a loved one's decision to identify as LGBTQ.

In *I Am Glad God Made Me a Girl*, young girls discover God's design and purpose for them. The story also touches on the reasons some girls believe becoming a boy makes sense for them. This resource shows girls that they are fearfully and wonderfully made by God and that as females, they are beautiful, kind, brave, smart, and strong.

The Boy Who Liked Tea Parties gently explores ways families can guide a child toward healthy gender identity and development. It is a valuable tool for parents, pastors, and counselors who seek to demonstrate love and compassion as they help children develop gender confidence.

www.ingramcontent.com/pod-product-compliance
Lightning Source LLC
LaVergne TN
LVHW041228080426
835508LV00011B/1108